Mother Blessings:

Honoring Women Becoming Mothers

Anna Stewart

Blessings!

Published by WovenWord Press
811 Mapleton Ave.
Boulder, CO 80304
www.wovenword.com

ISBN 0-9766678-0-0
ISBN13 978-0-9766678-0-3
LCCN 2005939206
1. Family and relationships 2. Motherhood 3. Pregnancy and childbirth
4. Birth celebrations 5. Creative projects

To my mother
who blessed me
daily
with her love

Contents

Section V: Preparing Body, Mind and Soul

Blessing Circle Foreword

A Blessingway for Mother Blessings

I invited seven friends and associates to join me in a virtual Blessingway. I asked them to imagine us all in sacred circle, gathered to bestow their blessings on this book and on me. I asked these women to join me as I took my creative project out into the world. I hoped for some sweet sentences of support. I got so much more. Caron shares the journey of our personal and professional worlds joined at the heart. Melissa reflects on the essence of this book—being together in community. Donna echoes the longing so many share for meaningful recognition of the process of becoming mothers. Rita reflects my belief in art as healer. Lisa reminds me that we all come to the room with wounds, and the very act of arriving can transform us. Annette writes about how we walk our own paths throughout all the seasons of our lives. And Gwen describes the power of community in creative expression. This foreword is a glorious example of how Blessingways are a powerful experience for all the women in the circle.

I walked into a festive, talkative group of women who gathered for a Blessingway ceremony for my thirty-five-year old girl friend, pregnant for the first time. In scanning the wise and happy faces around the room, I saw Anna, sitting quietly and watching. She returned my smile with her own, and as I sat down next to her on a soft pillow, I asked her to explain to me about a Blessingway, as this was my first one.

I listened to her calm and steady voice speaking of how a Blessingway ceremony supports a woman through pregnancy with friendship and caring conversations from women who have been there. I recalled my own painful pregnancy and difficult delivery as I participated in the ceremonies for my friend, wishing I'd had this for myself. How I would have loved to hear other women's honest stories about their struggles, and heart-felt stories about their connection with their child. As a pregnant professional woman, I went through it alone because I didn't know how to reach out. I dreamed of my daughter, but kept it my quiet secret. Anna explained that many women dream of their children. This one Blessingway ceremony and the fortuitous connection with Anna became my personal blessing.

Anna and I developed a wonderful friendship that has focused on helping women see the beauty of conscious childbirth and preparing themselves to enjoy it fully. I asked her to be a co-author on a pregnancy book. I have watched in admiration as this excellent writer went through her own birthing process to finally finding a home for this wonderful book. At last, the birthing is finished, and this gift to every pregnant woman is available.

Anna's writing from her personal heart honors women's innate, inherited ability to know how to give birth, reconnecting each woman to her inner wisdom. Anna helps women prepare for a conscious birth by being aware of their feelings, thoughts, and intuition through a variety of creative activities.

Yet there is a more profound reason for buying and sharing Anna's book with other woman, and creating a Blessingway for your friend or sister. One trait that sets women apart from men is their unique need to support one another through providing community. This is found in research on cancer support groups and moms' groups. A Blessingway ceremony is a supportive, joyful way to share the joy of pregnancy and birthing. A Blessingway gives depth to the pregnancy experience, far beyond sharing shower gifts, by offering personal testimonials and honest wisdom. A Blessingway is a ceremony for sharing blessings, one friend to another.
—Caron Goode, author of *Nurture Your Child's Gift* and owner of The Academy for Parent Coaches International

Mother Blessings is a gift to us all, to the children who will create our future, to the fathers who ideally bring warmth of heart to every family, to the mothers who open wide to allow life to pour through them, and to our many generations of ancestors who both birthed and died before us. Anna lovingly weaves together age-old and contemporary rituals and practices that give any and every family inspiration about how to welcome life in positive ways. She steps respectfully into our homes, honoring our many ways for worship, for celebration, for being together in

community. This book invites us all to remember the miracle of life and the value of slowing down to connect with one another and ourselves during this major life passage. The material is universal. And, the pages are generously filled with specific tools and practices, supporting the most novice or seasoned of parent. Every child deserves to be welcomed by devoted community. Every family needs a circle of witness and support as their children arrive. Every parent thrives in a field of love, the most fundamental nourishment for the long journey ahead. This book sets the stage for a lifetime of parenting in conscious collaboration with the sacredness in all. Anna is feeding the future with this book, reminding us to pause, listen, connect, and enjoy the blessed gifts of life . . . together.
—Melissa Michaels, social artist, Wild Life Productions

Pregnancy, birth, and motherhood are profoundly important to me. In my first two pregnancies, I did not have the opportunity to have a Blessingway, or maybe I didn't quite know what one was, or how to have one.

When I was faced with the likelihood that my third pregnancy would be my last, I needed to honor that in a deep way. I wanted to celebrate the life within me and the imminent birth, but also to recognize the profound impact pregnancy and birth had had on my life, and to accept the end of my childbearing. I needed a spiritual, powerful, ceremony with support from family and friends.

I didn't quite know where to begin; neither did the people closest to me. I wish I had had Anna's book at that time. It is exactly what I needed. Fortunately, my midwife had conducted simple Blessingways before. She helped me and my family decide what elements we wanted, and she offered to lead it. Each person lit a candle with his or her blessing. We collected the candles together in a ceramic bowl with sand and lit them again during my labor. How amazing to see those flames during labor, their passion and love lighting the way for my son. Each person also brought a flower. I have those dried flowers today. My son is six years old and I still look back on that blessing as a source of support for his life and our family.

I have known Anna for many years. We have grown closer since the birth of our youngest children through our unique mothering experiences. Both of our children have special needs. When Anna shared with me that she was writing this book, I was thrilled. Many women, like myself, are drawn to the idea of a Blessingway, yet they don't know where to begin. This book will help women and their families create personalized, meaningful ceremonies. Ultimately, it will support them in their transition to motherhood and in welcoming a new child. Anna and I both know so well that the unexpected can happen. Each child comes into the world with unique gifts and challenges. Rituals honoring motherhood give babies and their parents strength and a steady foundation to both face those challenges, and to deeply experience the joy of parenting. This kind of beginning, in turn, helps to create stronger communities and a more peaceful world.

Anna is a person who uses her skills to create community, to support families, and to encourage creativity in others. I am grateful to be her friend and grateful that she has chosen to do the important work of writing a book about mother blessings; it is a gift to us all. It is with my devoted friendship and sense of unity in creating a better world, that I give my blessing to Anna and her wonderful new book.
—Donna Wilson, social worker

I am honored that my art is a part of this book. I love how Anna has incorporated art and creativity with the important passages of our lives.

Art is an amazing thing. It has many facets and forms. It can simply provide for us something to do on a rainy day, it can help us express our love for each other in the form of a thoughtful gift, or it can become a profound tool of healing.

I personally have experienced the profound healing of art. Its process has taught me many things.

One thing that I have learned is that if I want to create something unique and authentic, the creative process demands that I work from a personal and honest place inside myself. The more I am willing to work from that state of consciousness, the more powerful the artwork becomes. In order to reach this level of honesty it is vital that I search inside myself with compassion and non-judgment; if I look inward with judgment and criticism instead, I end up only feeling self-defensive, which leads me to shut down rather than open up. It is also important that I bring all the wisdom that I have collected through my spiritual studies into my inner exploration. For it is with my wisdom that I will recognize the things inside of myself that need to be changed and to know how to change them.

As I begin a journey inward, I see many things. I see my strengths, passions, and desires. I see my weakness, flaws, and vulnerability. I see my thoughts and expectations. I see my lies and my truth. The more I look, the more I see. And with what I see, I examine, question, and understand more about myself. My story becomes clearer. I begin to understand the reasoning and logic behind my choices. And by developing this understanding, I now have the ability to accept my life as it is because I now realize that I did the best that I could with it. And I can also see that there is no longer any reason for self-hatred, shame, guilt, and regret, for I see that my flaws are not who I am. They are only my natural instincts and learned behaviors trying to help me survive and cope in a sometimes painful world. With this clarity and compassion I am now able to shift and transform, because those overpowering energies of self-hatred, shame, guilt and regret no longer have the hold on me they once did. My mind is now free to explore and learn healthier ways of thinking and being. And with everything I learn, it becomes the inspiration for another painting.

After learning to look inward with compassion and non-judgment, I realized that the creative process is a model that teaches me how to love and nurture myself. The way the creative process does this is that it gives me a setting and a reason with each painting I paint: to listen to my feelings, to question, explore and understand my feelings, to encourage myself, to make time for myself, to consider my ideas important, to realize my ability, to trust my judgment, to be patient with myself, to explore my potential and to allow myself to speak. All that self-nurturing and self-love is, the creative process has allowed me to experience. And now that I know what self-nurturing and self-love feels and looks like, I am able to expand and incorporate self-nurturing and self-love into the rest of my life.

I offer my blessing to this beautiful book and I wish for everyone who reads it that they will be inspired to create from their heart a memorial of love dedicated to the journey of another or their own.
—Rita Loyd, cover artist

I am so honored to have received this invitation to participate in the blessing of Anna's book on Mother Blessings. Not a mother myself, and having come from a very violent and broken down home, Anna's invitation has stirred great emotions and profound recollections of my own life. I've struggled to understand what I want to say in honoring my dear friend Anna in celebration for her book. The struggle is not because of any lack of words for Anna, and how she stands in her life. I have known her from our early twenties, and I have known her clarity in her roles as mother, as daughter, as friend, as professional. She is a dear friend and a truly amazing mother. No, my struggle is a personal struggle regarding birth and family.

As I've sat with Anna's invitation, I've come to realize that I have enjoyed motherhood through the woman-bonding of my friends, all mothers themselves. Perhaps I've been drawn to them for the mothering they give that my own mother did not. I have listened deeply to their detailed stories, describing their children. I have reflected on my own life as I visit friends and family and their children, watching how it is to be lovingly mothered. I have shared late-night girl talks and seen how reflecting on their children motivates them to change so they can mother at their very best.

I have taken their blessings and experiences with me to honor my own life. Through my own mindful determination, I have sought to create my own family and make it healthy, real, and truly happy. I also know that all of us have some pain or hurt from our own childhoods—that is life. Though I know my mother friends want to protect their children from harm, they also know that denying pain only creates suffering. Like birth and childhood, it is usually painful to become who we are.

Though I have been uncertain as to the direction my heart would send words out from this invitation, I am certain that the ritual of blessing motherhood is the beautiful imperative to the beginning of that

determination of honor and awareness. Through the intentional awareness, we learn to honor ourselves as whole people first, then as women and mothers. By honoring the woman who has given way to the mother-to-be, yielding to that new thing, she is expanded. It does not matter if it is her first child or her third child or her adopted child. That is, in fact, the bond we as women offer, whether through birth or simple extension of our selves. And to honor it, through deliberate ritual and celebration, is beautiful and self-affirming. It is, as Anna has offered, indeed necessary.
—Lisa Harrawood, community-focused businesswoman

I am grateful in knowing Anna and celebrating with her the expression of beauty in raw form. Witnessing together an awareness of what is, and creating from this awareness a way to see and feel more of the beauty that life offers, is a Blessingway.

I know Anna through our heartfelt experiences as mothers of children with different abilities. We have worked, cried, and played together sharing our commitment for inclusion of all children in our schools and community.

In thinking about how Anna has enriched my life, I thought of the alpine spring I saw high in the mountains this summer. The water flows out because it is there. It finds a way in the rock and soil because it must. It responds to its changing path in a flexible way. It reflects light and absorbs shadows as the forces of light and dark present themselves. And it just goes on and on because it is a source of life. In finding its way it is free and steady. In much the same way, coaxing intention to light gives form to the heart of our lives. Listening to what we need or see presents our way. Coming together to honor this nurtures our ability to draw strength in our lives as we go on and on.

Offering my blessing here has in itself been a gift. I wish to honor the beauty of Anna's commitment to life, and I share her deeply felt celebration of life's passages. We have had the joy of creating art together in community and seeing it grow bigger than ourselves.
—Annette Stewart, social activist

I believe that each and every one of us is born as a creative spirit. It is our natural desire to give form to our experience. This form can take on as many expressions as there are people in the world! Through song, dance, art, and craft, these forms do not only speak to who we are and what has meaning to us, but are also powerful ways of creating a meaningful connection between individuals. Forms of creative expression serve to communicate ideas, dreams, feelings, and beliefs from one to another.

Perhaps you have had the experience in which you view a piece of art or craft and it moves you in an inspiring way, conjuring up a new thought or giving you a different perspective. Maybe you have made your own art to process an experience, symbolize a transition in your life, or to offer as a gift. Awakening and connecting to the creative within you is profound. It serves to bring you back home to your true nature. By engaging in the actual process of creation and then experiencing the fruits of your labor, you will know the transformational powers of creative expression—to heal, inspire, understand, grow, and thrive in your life.

In my own life, I experienced a serious disconnect from the creative within me. Though my life was incredibly packed with activity, it lacked passion, color, and vibrancy. Because I had felt a slow death occurring within me, a flatness that I couldn't describe, I began to pursue my own awakening by re-entering college at thirty-three after experiencing a painful divorce. During this time, I recalled my childhood belief that I was an artist and wondered where that enthusiasm for art had gone. While on my journey, I discovered that what I was missing was something that had once been a vital part of my life as a child—art in community. I vividly remember sitting around a table creating with the weight of twenty-six moving elbows. Little did I know that when I created art with my sisters and brothers, I was acting out of the inherent drive to create!

In college I rediscovered that the act of creating with others provided a safe place for me to grow. I was able to see how my disregard for creative expression was blocking my own growth and healing. It was through the process of creative expression that I was able to tap in to the experience of life; I healed and awakened to my authentic self.

My own experience has led me to the conviction that we all must engage daily in creative expression through art, song, dance, words, movement, gardening, play and work, among others! It is critical to the success of the process that we play in community. Through shared experience, we gain encouragement, inspiration, new perspectives and understandings that cannot be had in solitude.

And here, we are fortunate to have heart-full Anna Stewart, a wise woman who knows such things and speaks to the same truth from her own experience and from her own conviction. To willingly and creatively engage in life with these tools is to experience a fulfilling life. Creative expression enables you to live fully—with passion, color and vibrancy. Thank you, Anna, for helping us all to wake up to our creativity!
—Gwen Thelan, artist and creativity coach

Introduction:

Honoring the Mother

"What?" he cried when he saw the home pregnancy test lying on the dining room table. "Already?"

We got pregnant the first time we tried much to my husband's disappointment.

I had already called my mom with the news in between pacing around the house. "I'm pregnant!" I told the cat. Then, "Oh my God, I'm pregnant," I screamed at the cat.

And that's what pregnancy is like. One second we feel such intense joy, our heart grows two sizes. The next we are scared to death.

I'd go to a prenatal appointment and be proud of my perfect weight gain and then I'd think, "Oh no, I don't know how to use a car seat."

It got worse. My prenatal screen for AFP3 came back elevated, which meant there was a chance I was carrying a child with Down syndrome. I was visiting my mother when the doctor called to schedule the amniocentesis. After a few more "Oh-my-gods," I did what mothers all over the world have done and still do with their babies. I talked to him. "Okay, my dear, I think you're just fine however you are, and we're going to take this test so that Daddy and everyone else knows that. Let me know if you need anything."

We barely spoke as we drove to the hospital. I was too busy talking to my baby—my first, but not my last, experience of comforting my child. I was also comforting myself. Maybe it was just denial, but I was sure my baby was fine.

Though my bladder ached (part of the deal is you have to have a full bladder), I was cheerful throughout the procedure. And I was fine for nine more days until the day before we were going to get the results. Then I let my fear get to me and I wondered how I would handle it if my child were born with a disability.

My son was fine. (Though two babies later I did have a baby with special needs, and she's fine, too, but that's another story).

The other thing I did—which women all over the world are doing—is I had a gathering of women. I had never heard of the term

"Blessingway," so my sister and I called it a baby shower. We ate my mother's chicken salad and passed around a polished crystal so each participant could imbue it with her loving words. We sang Irish lullabies and made a collage out of old photos and pictures and words from magazines. I laminated it and my son used it as a play-mat when he was a baby.

That simple ceremony, in the house I grew up in, changed my attitude. I had always been a "do-it-myself" kind of girl and I figured I'd be just fine doing the mom thing. But having to face my child's mortality made me think that, perhaps, I wanted people waiting on the shore when my ship came in. I wanted to know that they would feed me, hold me, or drive me to the doctors if I asked. After the Mother Blessing I knew that they would listen to me all night if I needed it, and I knew, more than anything, that they loved my baby. Thank the stars, because about that time I was starting to realize that I was going to have to have this baby alone, just like every women, every where, for all time. For the first time in my adult life, I knew I needed to allow myself to really trust my family and friends.

Part of me liked the secret inner life I held —I daydreamed about my child who danced within my womb. I wondered what he would look like, be like, and taste like. I loved that he shared my heart, my blood, even my ice cream.

And part of me was terrified. Never having seen a birth, or even a naked pregnant women, I had no idea how much my body would change. But the inner changes were much more alarming than my swollen feet and aching back. What were we thinking when we decided to have a baby? Why hadn't anyone told me about the huge change I was about to go thorough? I knew just enough to be sure it would change my life.

My husband spent most of that first pregnancy mourning. Every time we would go out to a fancy dinner or meet friends for a spontaneous hike, he'd come home and say, "Well that's the end of that." It drove me crazy. Not only because it made me think he was having major second thoughts, but because I knew that losing private, *couple* time was going to be the least of the changes we were about to experience. "My god, man," I wanted to yell at him, "We are going to die!" *Who cares about dinner,* I thought to myself as I snacked on yet another plate of cheese and crackers.

I was not depressed, remember—I was ecstatic; and also acutely aware that I had entered a portal, like a secret doorway my pregnancy had the key to unlock. I hadn't even seen the door before, but I could tell that women who'd given birth had been through it. They had gone through the portal of birth and emerged as mothers. And, like I was about to do myself, they had entered the portal alone, stepping into the unknown, hovering between life and death, boldly going where no man has ever gone. They, literally—we, literally—hold life in our hands. And not one of us is ever the same again.

Though we prefer to put a pink dress over the fact that pregnant women are experiencing a life in transition, when you're pregnant you *know* it. Although women have been giving birth for eons, each woman has to face the journey alone, and for some women this is a frightening realization. Pregnancy is a vulnerable time —on the edge between life and death. It's physically unsettling. It brings many women close to the world of "spirits" or the feminine mystery.

In *Grandmothers of the Light*, Paula Gunn Allen talks about birth being the most important event in a woman's life. It is her ticket into the adult woman's world:

> Having traversed the borderland between life and death in childbirth, she is welcomed and instructed in the woman's way. She learns the discipline of sacrifice—her body, time, nutrients, psyche, knowledge, skills, social life, relationships, spiritual knowledge and values are called into the service of her children. This passage pushes her to reach beyond whatever limits she thought she labored within, making her stronger and wiser.

No wonder women want to be drugged during this rite-of-passage. It's a huge responsibility. It's the biggest event of our lives and we deserve more than a few handshakes and pacifiers. We deserve (at least as much as we need) to be honored for this incredible journey.

After having two more children and attending many meaningful ceremonies, I offer all of you a guidebook to honor every woman you know who is becoming a mother. You can create your own Mother Blessings. Some people use the name Blessingway from the Navajo, and I will use both. Blessingway is a broader term that also works well for parents who are adopting their children. Whether our children come to us or through us, we still go through the portal of parenthood.

Through an intentional ceremony, rich with personal significance, our family and friends offer their heartfelt blessings as they create a physical symbol of their wishes. Mother Blessings focus on giving emotional support, commitment to being in community with the new family, and a deeper appreciation for the life-change that follows a baby's arrival.

Karen Robinson, a doula (birthing assistant for the mother) in Colorado, made a quilt with her friends and family at her Blessingway. "Not having had a Blessingway for my first baby, I really wanted one to help me deepen the experience of bringing a child into the world. The Blessingway was a way for me to connect with the collective spirit of women and mothers around the world and through the ages who have gone through the fire to bring a new life into being. It helped me remember that all of my female ancestors had successfully given birth and that I would too. It also strengthened the bond I had with the women in the room with me. I knew that I could count on them to help me with anything I needed, especially afterwards during the period of adjusting to being a mother of two."

As Karen reminds us, Mother Blessings are about honoring the mother (and father or partner) for taking on the responsibility of protecting and ensuring our futures. Every pregnant woman represents our sacred connection to one another, in our past, present, and future. Strangers are drawn to our bellies, not because of who we are individually, but because of what we represent collectively. They give bad advice, not because they want to scare us, but because they want to support us. (Well sometimes they want to scare us but only because they too, stood on the threshold between life and death and wondered how in the heck they were going to make it.)

My focus is first to come together with intention; secondly, to listen to and respond to what the guest-of-honor needs as she goes through this rite-of-passage. And third, it is to make something beautiful as a community.

We need ceremonies to remind us of these transitions. We need ceremonies to feel part of community and, most importantly, to express our hopes and fears, our dreams and worries, in a ritualized form. Cultures across the world mark special events—menses, marriage, childbirth, war, journeys, death—with ceremonies and rituals. They provide a formal way to understand the changes we are in the midst of, they give us a structure to make sense of the chaos within, and they offer a way to find inner peace and balance. They bring us together to celebrate, honor, and support our loved ones.

Blessingway is simply the name of one kind of ceremony. All of the examples and suggestions I offer you in this book can be used to mark many kinds of life events. You can plant a tree when a grandparent dies. You can make a banner with your friends at your wedding. You can make a necklace for a girl after she goes through puberty. You can make a personal box on your 50th birthday.

Mother Blessings is written for anyone who wants to create a meaningful ceremony to honor a woman as she becomes a mother. This book, my gift to you, provides everything from wording on invitations to instructions on making birth necklaces to deciding whom to invite. It makes it easy for anyone to host a Blessingway. It helps you figure out what elements are important to you, including bringing in your personal religious or spiritual beliefs, to make each ceremony a unique, personal, and meaningful event. Its focus is first to come together with intention; secondly, to listen to and respond to what the guest-of-honor needs as she goes through this rite-of-passage. And third, it is to make something beautiful as a community.

Creating art together gives us an opportunity for play. It helps us reconnect with the innate joy in making things. It reconnects us with the child within as we prepare to guide the child about to be born to us. It is a delightful reminder of how much fun it is to get down on the floor and get our hands dirty. It is immensely satisfying to gaze upon a product of our own hands. Making something gives form to our wishes, our blessings, and our love. When we do it together, it becomes bigger than all of us—it becomes a synergistic symbol of all the qualities we share with each other.

The stories I've included have been gathered over the years. I've changed names, rearranged events, and melded different occasions in order to be clear and in honor of the truth. So though not every story is true, all are very real.

I've "officiated" at Blessingways, attended as a guest, and been honored with three of my own. Next to my bed, on the wall above where my daughter slept for years, hangs a piece of driftwood from a beach in California with a rainbow of ribbons streaming down it. Tied to the ribbons are boughs of lavender, lace, a small stuffed Indian elephant and other handmade ornaments. My favorite one is not the most beautiful—it's a piece of cardboard with pink ribbons glued on. But it is the most meaningful. My mother made it, the first thing she had ever made me and sent to me in Colorado when I was pregnant with my third child. Every time I dust the ribbon of blessings, my heart swells inside me, and I say a silent blessing of gratitude for the circle of friends and family that still surround my family.

I wore the necklace my friends made for my second child at his birth. He came only a few days after the Blessingway, in a rush to be born before Christmas. When I finally took off the necklace, weeks after his birth, I tied it to a redwood stick my husband and I had made for our wedding. A life-stick, it marks all our big life events.

And the crystal imbued with love from my first Blessingway, before I even knew what they were called, sits on my desk while I write this to you, reminding me of how we are all walking a path between worlds, between what is and what could be, between what we want and what we have, between what we love and what loves us.

May your pregnancies and gestations of hope, be filled with satisfying love, deep connection, and delightful laughter.

I

THE BLESSINGWAY CEREMONY

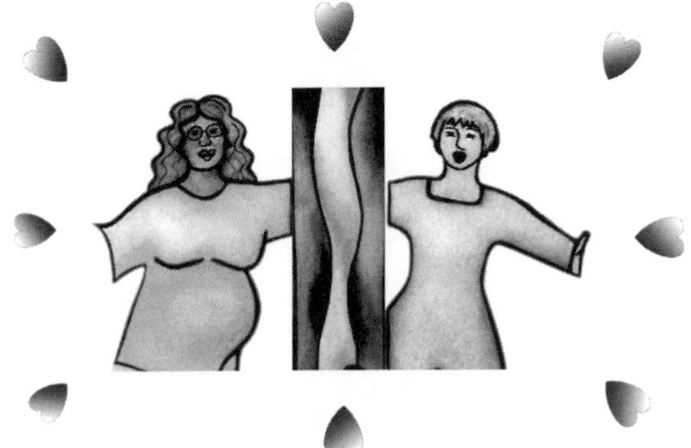

Jenna's Mother Blessing

Every Mother Blessing is a uniquely personal event. There is no right way to do one; there is only your way. Immerse yourself into Jenna's ceremony to experience the power, the beauty, and the joy of a Blessingway.

When Jenna lies in bed at night and touches her belly, she can feel her baby moving. *Is that really my baby?* she wonders. As excited as she is, other lonely thoughts creep into her mind: *Can I give birth without drugs? Will I like being a mother? I've always wanted to be a mom. I will love it! Won't I? Yes, I'll just want to stay home and snuggle with my baby. But what if I get bored? What if I can't do it?*

Jenna confides in her best friend Beth. "I'm feeling so lonely," she tells her. "Hardly anyone I know has had a baby. What if I lose all my friends? I'll go crazy."

As Beth listens to Jenna, she wonders how to help her friend. She doesn't understand Jenna's fears, but she does understand that she needs support and reassurance.

"Have you ever heard of a Blessingway, Jenna?" she asks. Jenna shakes her head. "We did one for my sister, Miranda, when I went back to visit my family last summer. It was really great. I thought it was going to be some hippie thing but it turned out to be a beautiful ceremony. Miranda was getting really nervous about being a mom. She sounded a lot like you. She said she felt much better afterwards. She's doing great. Maybe we should do one for you."

Jenna looked at Beth. "What do I have to do?"

"Leave it to me. I wanted to throw you some kind of party, but a shower just didn't seem meaningful enough," Beth said. "Let's start with the easy part. You're due in five weeks so we should have the Blessingway two weeks from now, that's the fifteenth. Since most of your friends work in the day, let's do a potluck dinner. I'll ask Louise to help me with flowers and decorations—she loves that stuff, and Sue can bake one of her famous chocolate cakes for desert."

"But now the big question—what do you need, Jenna? "

"I'm not exactly sure," Jenna told her. "I guess I want to feel that my friends won't abandon me. I want to feel that they won't be afraid to talk to me, or hold the baby, or just listen to me. I'm scared of being alone with a baby and I'm afraid I won't seem as smart or interesting once I'm a mom."

Jenna took a deep breath, "More than anything, I'm afraid I won't be a good mother."

Beth took Jenna's hand, "I know you'll be a great mom, but I think we can help. Tell me who you want to invite. Who do you feel comfortable sharing this part of yourself with and who do you think will be able to offer you real support?"

Once they came up with a guest list and finalized the time, Beth sent invitations written on hand-made paper that said:

Jenna's Blessing
Please join Jenna and her baby in celebrating her journey to motherhood with a Blessingway. Our intention is to surround Jenna with our loving support along with our heartfelt wishes for a safe and fulfilling birth.
Please bring a potluck dish to share, and your written blessings.
Call Beth if you have any questions at 111-2222
September 15th, 6 to 8 pm at 12 Blooming Lane

Jenna's Blessingway, on a warm fall day, began at dusk. It was the perfect metaphor for the transition Jenna was making from woman to mother. Pillows and a rocking chair were set up in a tight circle.

Jenna's husband, Steve, greeted the women, and then graciously left. In the middle of the living room candles flickered on a small table decorated with fresh flowers and a picture of Jenna's parents, to remind Jenna of her own happy childhood. There was also a beautiful heart-shaped amethyst stone that her husband gave her on their first anniversary. Beth suggested that she use it during the Mother Blessing ceremony to hold all the love her friends have for her. "It's also just the right size to grip during labor," Beth told her.

Jenna loved having all her women friends in one place. She was excited to share her pregnancy with them, and she was a little nervous about what would happen. (Beth assured her that they would not be sampling baby food or making bets on her due date.)

The women talked for a while, some catching up, and others introducing themselves. Then the women sat in a circle, the custom for Mother Blessings. Sitting in a circle allows everyone to see each other, and the guests to be seen as equals. The mother-to-be often sits in a cushioned chair, as a place of honor and of comfort. Some women sit in chairs, some sit on the floor. Jenna felt uncomfortable asking her friends to wash her feet or brush her hair, activities done in the Navajo Blessingways. But one of her friends, Erin, was a massage therapist, and she gently slipped Jenna's foot in her lap and started massaging her feet with lavender oil. Jenna gratefully accepted the attention and sighed with contentment. " Oh, that feels so good," she told Erin. Another friend brought her a steaming mug of raspberry tea.

When everyone was seated and quiet, they held hands, forming a circle. "As we gather here today in this circle of sisters, we come to bless our friend Jenna as she goes from being a woman to a mother. We thank all our sisters, mothers, and grandmothers, some in spirit, that join us. We hold the intention that our voices are true and our hearts pure. Blessed be," Beth said, starting the ceremony.

The blessings began, each woman sharing her love for Jenna. Each friend told her how she felt, what blessings she wished for her and her baby, and the gifts she had brought to their lives.

Beth, holding the heart crystal, began: "Jenna, we've known each other for six years now, ever since we met at that weird women's book group. I knew we'd be friends when we both rolled our eyes at the suggestion that we read comic book erotica for the next discussion. You've been such a great friend to me, Jenna, and I am so grateful to have you in my life." Beth took a deep breath. "You've always made me feel good about myself, even when I can't believe what a doofus I am. That ability, to see the good in others, even when they can't, will make you a wonderful mother. And that is my blessing for you, to always remember your heart and how much love you have to share. I promise to remind you of this whenever you're feeling low. I love you, and I can't wait to see you become a mother—you're going to be great."

Beth stood up to give Jenna a hug. "Thank you, " was all Jenna could say. Beth gave Monica, sitting beside her, the crystal. Monica pulled out a blue note card. "I was too nervous to do this without writing it down, " she said. "Jenna, thank you for sharing this beautiful journey with me. I am truly honored to see you grow so richly in your new role as a woman and a mother. My blessing for you is the moon and the stars, may they never be far from your reach." She put down the card and looked at Jenna, "Beth is right, Jenna, you are going to be an amazing mom. I can just see you taking your baby out for moonlit walks and finding new constellations in the sky. Your baby is blessed to have you for a mother."

Each woman held the polished heart-shaped amethyst stone as she spoke. The women cried and laughed together as they shared their heartfelt wishes and blessings. Each woman wrote her blessings in a spiral-bound blank book. Jenna added photos, entries, and the birth story later.

After everyone shared, Jenna spoke. "Thank you all for being here. When Beth first suggested this I wasn't sure I could do it, even though I really needed to know that you would stand by me. I couldn't tell if I was more afraid of losing you or of becoming a mother. Now I know you'll be here. So now, I'm just afraid of motherhood." She smiled, trying to show she was kidding. Her friends waited for her to continue.

Jenna picked up the picture of her parents. "I think what I'm really afraid of is that I won't be as good a mother as my mom. She was the perfect mom. She was always there when I got home from school. She took us to cool places. She read to us every night. She even let us dance in the rain. I don't know if I can really be a good mother to this baby." Jenna held her belly.

Debbie walked over to Jenna, "I can tell you right now that you won't be like your mother, you'll be like you. I had a lot of the same worries when I was pregnant. At first, I listened to all the advice around me, but that just overwhelmed me even more. I decided just to listen to my baby and myself. Now, no matter what I am worried about—whether it's starting solids or if I should be letting him play more with other kids, I ask myself whether or not what I am doing comes from love or expectation. If I'm doing something because someone else says I should, then it's expectation. If it comes from love, I know it's the right thing."

Jenna could only nod as her emotions surged through her. "Thank you Debbie, thank you all. I feel so loved right now. I can't tell you how much this means to me."

"And I don't know if you know how much this means to me, " Beth said. "I feel so much closer to everyone." The other women murmured their agreement.

"Don't forget the presents, Beth! " Erin chimed in.

Beth looked at Jenna. "We decided that we wanted to get you something that would really help you. So we decided to set up a food tree for after the baby comes. Someone will bring you and Steve dinner every night for the first three weeks. We want you to rest, be with your new family, and be nourished by your friends."

Before Jenna could respond, Debbie stood up with a big box in her hands, "And since we know you love to read, we each got you a copy of one of our favorite children's books. Your sister and parents sent one too—they even recorded themselves reading the story on a tape."

Jenna laughed as she looked through the box. "Oh I love these," she said, "*Horton Hears a Who* is one of my favorites. And *Goodnight Moon* and *The Little Engine that Could*!"

"This is great. Thank you," Jenna said as she made eye contact with each friend.

Before they got up to eat cake, Stephanie started a song, encouraging everyone to join her:

"Jenna, you are beautiful.
Jenna, you are strong.
A unique and special woman,
You've been perfect all along,
Jenna, you are beautiful."

The women commented to one another about how nourished they felt. Women who had never met before this night hugged each other like sisters before they headed home.

The ceremony was over, but the blessings had only begun to work their magic.

Jenna's labor began a week after her Blessingway. The candles and flowers were still on the table, along with the crystal heart and blessing book. While she waited to be sure she was in labor, she held the crystal and thought about her friends' blessings for her and her baby. She was still holding the crystal when Steve came home. When he walked in he looked at her and said, "Hi mom," and Jenna felt the truth of her new role as she felt her body giving birth, not only to her baby, but to herself as the mother she was ready to be.

History of the Blessingway

From the heart of Earth, by means of yellow pollen
Blessing is extended.
Blessing is extended.
On top of a pollen floor may I there in blessing give birth!
With long life-happiness surrounding me
May I in blessing give birth!
May I quickly give birth!
In blessing may I arise again, in blessing may I recover,
As one who is long life-happiness may I live on!
—Navajo chant from the *Blessingway Ceremony*

Her belly is taut and full with her first child. She sits quietly, the girl becoming a mother, in the east part of the circle, the place of new beginnings.

Her hair is pinned in the shape of a butterfly, though soon it will be brushed and re-pinned by her mother into a bun, the hairstyle of the mother.

This is her Blessingway, a ceremony to offer blessings for a safe birth and a healthy baby and to honor her for the mother she is becoming. The Blessingway Singer sings a few songs, signifying the beginning of the ceremony. The mothers of the village give her a ritual bath of yucca suds while they sing and pray over her.

Though this is her first Blessingway, she has seen many others. Her people, the Navajo, conduct Blessingway ceremonies to bless the "one sung over." Through the Blessingway they bestow their wishes for good health, safe journeys, and protection from harm. It's a way to recognize each member of the community. Without new children, the community would die, so the Blessingway gives them a way to express gratitude and appreciation for the woman taking the risk of childbirth, and to celebrate the new life growing inside her. The Blessingway is the oldest ceremony in the Navajo society. Holy People held the first Blessingways when they created humankind. The Holy People taught humankind both rituals and skills. Changing Woman, the first mother, taught them the Blessingway ceremony and some Blessingway songs. Changing Woman married the Sun and their son slayed many of the monsters so that people could live safely on earth. Her name translates to "the woman who is transformed time and time again," a metaphor for a women's life cycle. She is the divine mother, a symbol of fertility, and the epitome of a good and wise mother.

The name, Blessingway, is really an understatement of the Navajo meaning. According to Leland Wynman, an expert in Navajo religion, the term encompasses everything that is interpreted as good, including qualities such as beauty, harmony, success, perfection, wellbeing, order, and ideals.

Historically, people had Blessingways for many life stages, including journeys, birth, and death. It was more common to have a Blessingway to welcome the new child after birth than to celebrate the pregnant woman. As the Native American culture started to catch on with non-Native Americans during the counterculture revolution of the 60s, people started to learn about sacred ceremonies. Alternative thinkers, especially those that looked for spiritual enlightenment without religious dogma, found themselves drawn to Native American ritual qualities. They started to incorporate activities such as sitting in circles, singing and chanting together, along with adding purification rites such as smudging with sage or sweet grass (these herbs are tied together and burned, creating a cleansing smoke), and ritualistically washing and grooming the honoree. They, like the Navajo, liked the feeling of honoring individuals within their communities. They discovered that everyone benefited from such ceremonies. It was a natural progression to begin giving Blessingways for those in major life transitions. And so the contemporary Blessingway or Mother Blessing was born. Because the essential elements are so simple (intention, gathering, blessing) it is expected that each ceremony will be different, each will be unique, and each will have personal meaning.

Though a ceremony is a beautiful way to mark a rite-of-passage, it is worth noting the belief system underneath the rituals. Native Americans, like many indigenous cultures, believe that pregnancy is a state of wellness, and birth is a natural process. It is not an illness, or a medical condition requiring a doctor. There is nothing wrong with a healthy, pregnant woman.

In all cultures, a pregnant woman does everything she can to ensure optimum health for herself and her baby. The community adds its support, and we, too, can use the support of our communities to create rituals such as the Blessingway ceremony, and weave a miraculous and organic life process with homage to our own ancestors and spirituality, along with recognition of our individual journeys of becoming mothers.

WHY MOTHER BLESSINGS?

Mother Blessings give women becoming mothers a safe environment where they can share their fears and excitement. A ceremony publicly honors a woman as she makes the transformation from woman to mother. It is a concrete symbol of her community's love and support. Each woman can get what she needs, as we can see in the following stories.

As a doula, Tia had attended several Blessingways. When it was her turn to be the center of attention, she knew she wanted to include movement, sacred rituals, and elements from the original Blessingway practiced by the Navajo Indians.

She asked her best friend, Juanita, to be the hostess, and they talked about what Tia wanted and needed. Though Tia understood the birth process and had supported many birthing mothers, she had not given birth herself. Juanita challenged Tia not to "manage" the ceremony, and to learn to let go and surrender to the process. Tia understood intellectually that the birth of her baby and her own passage into new motherhood would go more smoothly if she could trust herself and her friends to support her and honor her.

Juanita asked Tia to wear a skirt to her Blessingway. Since Tia was planning a homebirth, they held the Blessingway in her bedroom to fill it with their blessings and love. Nine women came, each bearing food, a candle, a written blessing, and a bead.

On a warm spring day, Tia's Blessingway began at dusk. Like Jenna's in the first story,. this symbolized the transition Tia would soon make from woman to mother.

Once all the women had arrived, Juanita asked them to line up outside the bedroom door with Tia in the front. In the doorway, Juanita lit a sage bundle and smudged Tia from her head to her toes, front and back, as a purification rite. She did the same to each woman. The cleansed women silently entered the bedroom and stood in a circle.

As they held hands, Juanita said, "Welcome to this Mother Blessing circle. We are here today to celebrate the birth of Tia and Jack's baby, and the birth of Tia as a mother.

"We open our hearts to this baby and his or her true home. May this baby's family and friends fill these rooms with their love, their support, and their blessings." She then welcomed each woman by name.

Juanita broke out of the circle to turn on a CD player, and played a beautiful song from one of Tia's favorite artists, Joanne Shenandoah. Juanita began dancing, swaying to the music. As she danced, she said, "I invite you all to open your hips and knees, wrists and shoulders. We honor our friend Tia through this ancient dance of opening as she prepares to open her body to allow her child to emerge. I asked Tia to wear a skirt so she could feel the flow of feminine energy coursing through her body and into the earth."

The women danced, swirling together as a concrete reminder that to give birth, a woman needs to trust her body's wisdom and to allow the divine energy she believes in to guide and protect her.

Tia said later, "I loved every part of my Mother Blessing, but my favorite moment was when we all danced together. I felt very vulnerable and exposed, but at the same time I felt totally safe and held. It was wild. There was a moment in my labor when the pressure of my daughter's head was so intense, I started to panic. My midwife, who had been at the Mother Blessing, put on the song we had danced to—I was instantly transported to the dance and suddenly I felt safe again and knew I could push her out."

Sarah also benefited from her Mother Blessing. Her friends each brought a candle. They shared their blessings with Sarah as each lit her candle and planted it in a large bowl filled with sand. "At the birth of my baby," Sarah explained, "during one of those moments of doubt, my eyes caught the light coming from the lit candles in the corner of the bedroom. The light was very powerful coming from all those candles, and I was immediately brought back into the circle of my friends' blessings, and into the circle of all women who had ever given birth throughout the eons of time. I felt all their energy with me, and I knew I could do it. And then I saw my midwife's daughter's small beeswax candle, and it was about an inch from burning down all the way. I still so distinctly remember seeing her candle, and promising myself that I would birth this baby before the candle burned out. So in calling in the love and power of all women, and especially my circle of friends, I birthed my baby boy, and the small candle was still burning."

Torrie found that her community deepened and grew when she had a Mother Blessing for her fourth child. Her family had recently moved into a new suburban neighborhood. When she was on bed rest for eight weeks in the middle of her pregnancy, her neighbors started to cook and clean for her. She was a little nervous about inviting them all to her Blessingway, as many had different religious beliefs than she did. With the support of her close friends and family, she opened her doors and heart and invited them all. The Mother Blessing gave Torrie a chance to thank them all for their generosity and support. When she saw how truly glad they were to help her and be with her throughout her pregnancy, she let go of her concerns and graciously accepted their loving presence in her life.

Jenny knew the greatest gift she could give her family was the experience of the Blessingway. "I felt somewhat shy to organize my own ceremony," she shares, "but knew how I wanted it to go. I knew I wanted my husband to be included, and I felt that the spirit associated with a family Blessingway would be the most important 'prenatal care' we could experience. I understood that the feelings attached to it would be a potential pattern for how we would experience the birth of our baby. As a Christian I wanted to sing sacred hymns and prayers to invite the spirit of Jesus.

"I prepared my altar with a picture of Jesus, a bag of wheat grass, a jar of kamut and flax seeds, and a cloth diaper. We had requested that no one bring gifts, but rather donate to our cloth diaper fund. Our friends gave generously and I was able to order all of the diapers I needed.

"As each family arrived, I had a feeling of perfection. These were the very souls we were destined to bless the way with!

"My friend, Nancy, offered a wonderful prayer of thanksgiving and protection to start the ceremony. Rico, another friend, told the history of the Blessingway, describing how the Navajos physically prepared, through ritual touch, the one who was honored to receive the blessing. And my dear friend, Jeannine, described the purpose of passing around a length of yarn, which we all wound around our wrists to symbolize community. As we wound the string I sang a hymn.

"Jeannine and Rico did the ritual touch. She let down my hair and noted coming wisdom —my first gray hairs. Paul, my husband, said he must be very wise, as his head is covered in gray. Then Rico massaged Paul's shoulders and expressed to him his confidence in his roll as a husband and father/provider.

"Then they massaged our feet with a bottle of essential oil. As Jeannine massaged various reflex points, I felt a wave of loving energy wash over my body and the baby started to kick excitedly. Rico worked on Paul, and as they massaged I asked that my friends go around the circle telling who they were and how they knew our family. This was the highlight of the gathering for me. I found myself tearing up as expressions of love were conveyed to Paul and me.

"A feeling of love entered my heart for the circle of friends that had gathered around me and my eternal companion, Paul. We finished the party with a feast of fresh fruit and muffins, then visited and took pictures.

"From that moment until the baby arrived, we have been blessed and set apart for the important task of welcoming our child into our home."

Mother Blessing Program:

Along with loving intention, you'll need to do one thing in each of these categories to create a beautiful Mother Blessing.

- *Welcoming*
- *Opening the ceremony*
- *Nurturing the mother*
- *Offering your blessings*
- *Creating a symbol or talisman*
- *Completion*
- *Feasting*

Planning a Blessingway

With heartfelt intentions, a beautiful environment, and a commitment to support the mother or parents, Blessingways can be done any time and any place. Terry had her Blessingway in a private grove of redwoods with just three friends. They made a sculpture out of branches, lichen, pinecones, and small stones.

Susan had her Blessingway in her big kitchen. Paints, brushes, and small decorations were laid out on the newspaper-covered counters. Each woman was given a square of white cotton and asked to write or draw her blessing for Susan's first baby.

The basic elements necessary for a Blessingway are:

Intention

- ❖ How to know what you want
- ❖ Choosing a hostess

Container

- ❖ Creating invitations and deciding whom to invite
- ❖ Choosing time of day and location
- ❖ Deciding when during pregnancy
- ❖ Creating the environment: decorations, music
- ❖ Gifts

Symbol

- ❖ Create a gift together such as a necklace or a mobile
- ❖ Imbue a crystal or special object with blessings
- ❖ Share birth stories or qualities
- ❖ Make an altar

Program/schedule

- ❖ Welcoming
- ❖ Opening the ceremony
- ❖ Introductions
- ❖ Nurturing the mother
- ❖ Offering your blessings
- ❖ Creating a symbol
- ❖ Completion
- ❖ Feasting

KNOWING YOUR INTENTIONS

Before you can send out invitations, gather flowers, bake cakes, and light candles, you need to decide what kind of Blessingway you are going to create. You already know the reason for it, but ask the honoree (or yourself) what she needs from her friends and family.

The intention is the most important aspect of a Blessingway. It's not always easy to know what you want, and it's even harder to ask for what you need. To start understanding your intention, ask yourself these questions and write down your answers:

❖ **Whom do you want to invite?** As you make the list, consider the qualities you share with your friends. How do your friends make you feel? Safe? Wild? Comfortable? What do you and your friends like to do together? Sing, cook, read, be outside, pray? How many people do you have on your list? Do they all know each other? Does that matter to you?

❖ **What time of year is it?** How does this time of year make you feel? Some women become very private during the winter months and want to focus on warm foods and small gatherings. Others feel cooped up in winter and want to dance and sing and chase the cold away.

❖ **How do you feel about the following activities?**

- Foot washing, foot massages, painting toenails
- Smudging (using burning sweet grass or sage to symbolically purify)
- Dancing as a group
- Singing (being sung to, singing along with others, singing solo)
- Invocations, prayer, ritual
- Hosting a ceremony in your home
- Gifts

❖ **How do you want to welcome your baby?** Are you drawn to making a necklace, a quilt, clothes for you or the baby, sculptures, a belly mask (plaster cast of a pregnant belly), or having your friends put their handprints all over the baby's room? Would you prefer to plant a tree or make a simple blessing book? What other aspects of welcoming are important to you? Perhaps some of it is private, such as you and your partner writing a letter pledging yourselves to your child.

By answering these questions honestly you will begin to see what kind of ceremony best fits you, and then you can consider what else you need, such as a chance to share your fears and concerns, to ask for help or meals after the baby comes, or a chance to thank your friends and family.

Some women self-edit, and have difficulty asking for what they really want for fear of offending someone, or because they feel guilty asking for what they need. Both are common among women, especially mothers.

During the ceremony, ask the mother-to-be what she needs, and before you close, ask if she needs anything else.

Grace was concerned that some of her guest would be "weirded-out" by the Blessingway her close friends had planned for her. She felt an obligation to invite some of her neighbors who didn't share her religious or personal values. Her friend, Betsy, assured her that it wouldn't matte—that the women would only say things they felt comfortable saying, and no one would be asked to do something she didn't want to do. For Grace, it was a lesson in letting go and trusting her self and her friends. The Blessingway was deeply satisfying for all the women, including her seventy-four-year-old grandmother who had never been to anything like it.

Honoring the Woman

It is important for the mother-to-be, her friends, or the new parents welcoming a child through adoption, to allow themselves to experience the whole range of emotions that this life-changing event brings. Though a childless, single friend may not understand her friend's fears about losing her identity as she becomes a mother, or a new father's worries about financing his child's college fund, it's critical that she or he not censor or dismiss them. No one knows what it's like to become a parent until they have become one. And every parent does things differently. Pregnancy intensifies emotions, so give a pregnant woman lots of room to explore her feelings. While some women may need therapy, most just want their friends to listen and not judge. The Blessingway provides a safe structure to honor and witness this passage.

Although women have been giving birth for eons, each woman has to face the journey alone, and for some women this is a frightening realization. A good project for someone feeling this way is something tangible that can be worn during birth or used as a visual focusing tool during labor. The group can bead her a necklace, paint a large T-shirt or nightgown, or frame a photograph of all of them surrounding her, which the mother-to-be can keep by her bedside.

Some women want to bring in a spiritual element that may have been missing from their public experience of pregnancy, but may be living within their hearts. Some may want to honor Mother Nature or recognize the archetypal Mother. Creating a birth altar is a wonderful project for women seeking deeper meaning in their experience of pregnancy. Other ideas include planning a garden together (depending upon the season) or holding the ceremony in a special place outside.

Women or couples who are expanding their family through adoption often find the tree-planting ceremony, as well as creating a special book with blessings and wishes for the new family's future, very moving. Another idea is to create a series of blessing flags to hang out front or near a window so everyone can see there is reason to celebrate in that home.

A woman who finds pregnancy very sensual will likely enjoy making a belly mask. She might also like to have her shoulders massaged, her hair brushed, her feet washed in rose water, her toenails painted, and her belly painted or hennaed with intricate designs. A wild spirit may take things even further and have her friends massage her entire body with oils and scents as a symbol of the maidenhood she is leaving behind as she journeys into motherhood.

Choosing a hostess

You will also need to decide who is going to be the hostess. If you are pregnant and reading this, consider asking a friend who is comfortable with leading a group and whom you think would enjoy this. Desire is more important than experience.

Even if you don't have a friend ready to take this on, you can still have a meaningful ceremony with the help of this guidebook.

Sometimes good intentions are not enough—you need ideas, a focus, and a welcoming environment. Carmen had never been to a Blessingway—and neither had any of her friends—but she knew she wanted to have some kind of meaningful ceremony to welcome her baby. She invited her father, her husband, and two close friends. Her midwife offered to help but didn't have much more information than Carmen. They sat in a circle (no one thought of flowers or decorations) and the midwife said a few words about honoring Carmen and welcoming her baby. Each person offered a short blessing, and Carmen asked her husband to read a poem she liked. Then it was over. Though they all wanted to support Carmen, they didn't really know how to make her feel deeply cherished. And she didn't really know what she wanted, either. That's why it's so important to have a guide, including this book, to help create a truly meaningful and memorable ceremony.

By customizing your own welcoming ceremony, with or without help, you can host a Blessingway that no one in attendance will ever forget. Carmen's friends and family would have brought flowers, candles, and food if they had been asked, though none may have felt comfortable leading the ceremony. If you are pregnant and don't have anyone who wants to be the host, you can lead the event and ask your friends and family to do the rest. The heart of a Blessingway is the offering of the wishes and blessings, which involves everyone.

If you have a hostess, she needs to ask you what your needs are, and decide what elements she is comfortable incorporating, as discussed above. Just because the idea of having your feet washed in warm rose water is appealing to you, it may not be comfortable for her. Perhaps, instead, you might assign someone to greet the women as they arrive, and symbolically wash their hands in rose water to prepare them for the ceremony.

The Cast

These are roles to assign prior to the Mother Blessing.

- ***Messenger**: Sends invitations, handles RSVPs*
- ***Hearth-Tender**: Takes care of food and decoration arrangements*
- ***Conductor**: Leads, models, goes first for Blessingway elements*
- ***Cherisher**: Leads, supplies, models nurturing aspects (hair, feet, hands)*
- ***Scribe**: Writes down blessings, meanings and gifts during the ceremony*
- ***Singer**: Plans music, supplies instruments or words for songs, leads songs, chants, toning*
- ***Creatrix**: Plans, supplies, prepares, explains, models art project/activity*
- ***Postpartum Helper**: Organizes food tree, makes announcement for front door*

CONTAINER

A Mother Blessing is a series of rituals put together in an intentional way to create a ceremony. It is a process of building a safe, supportive container for a mother-to-be. When you have created a safe container by carefully choosing guests, having a beautiful and distraction-free home, setting clear boundaries of behavior, and a stated purpose of working together to support the honoree, you begin to fill your container with love, support, confidence, trust, commitment, and nourishment. A woman on the verge of becoming a mother can become all the qualities she receives from her sacred circle of loved ones. She embodies, and holds, through the physical things we offer her, a safe container to birth her child into the world.

A Mother Blessing focuses on the mother and not on the baby. It is a public acknowledgment of the hard work ahead of her as she labors, births, and welcomes her child. It is such a huge thing to become a mother: a truly life-changing journey. Through the Blessingway we can help our friends, sisters, daughters, and mothers prepare for it.

The Mother Blessing container has specific elements that all need to be considered.

- ❖ Choosing whom to invite and sending invitations
- ❖ Time of day, location, and length
- ❖ When during pregnancy
- ❖ Environment: decorations, music, scents
- ❖ Gifts
- ❖ Program

Whom to Invite

The easy answer to whom to invite is to only invite people who truly care about you, and with whom you can feel comfortable sharing yourself and your home. But most of us have a wider circle of people who are part of our lives.

Unless you have a relationship with a co-worker outside of work, I would not recommend inviting them to your Blessingway. It's a personal event, not a professional one. However, colleagues often do want to offer something for a pregnant peer. Diane's co-workers pooled funds and bought her a beautiful nightgown and robe. They gave it to her on her last day of work. They were all relieved they didn't have to host a baby shower in the break room.

What about husbands, fathers, or other men in a pregnant women's life? If your partner wants to be there and you want him to be there, then include him and give him part of the hosting duties. It's still rare for men to be included, but there's really no reason not to if everyone is comfortable with that situation. As a general guideline, I would not recommend inviting the husbands of your friends, unless you want more of a party, like Tina and Eric did for their adopted daughter (see adoption section).

One way men can participate is by doing the cooking and cleaning both before and after. It is a symbol of their new roles as caretakers.

Children, especially daughters, of the mother-to-be, love being included. It's a wonderful way to show young girls that having children is a normal part of life and something to be celebrated and not feared. In general they need to be old enough to sit and listen, so that the honoree isn't distracted with their squirming or questions. This event is intended to focus on the mother. If there are younger children who want to be included, you could invite them to come at the end of the ceremony and give their blessings.

Casual neighbors are not usually invited. However, some neighbors can become very close friends, and may be key people in birth plans.

Unless you have a personal friendship with your obstetrician, she or he would not be invited. However, due to the more intimate relationship midwives and doulas offer, they are often invited. Because they spend more time getting to know their clients and even meeting in their homes, they become key people for emotional support. Midwives often decline the invitations due to their workload, but I believe they appreciate the invitation.

Invitations

Ask any women who's been invited to a Blessingway, whether for an upcoming marriage, birth, birthday, adoption, menopause rite, or a goodbye ritual, and chances are she will say it was a wonderful ceremony. For some people, the invitation is their first encounter with a Blessingway, so make it reflect the event you envision.

For a very small circle of close friends a phone call is fine as an invitation, but written invitations create a stronger sense of purpose.

While store-bought invitations can work well, they need to have enough room to explain a Mother Blessing and what the participants should bring. The honored woman will likely keep one for her baby scrapbook.

Always include:

❖ The place (at the pregnant woman's home or somewhere else?)

❖ Whom to send RSVPs to (not the guest-of-honor)

❖ The date and time (pregnant women get tired so consider her state)

❖ A brief description of the ceremony (is it a potluck dinner or an afternoon tea? Will it be indoors or outside?)

❖ What to bring (food, candles, flowers, objects for the projects)

Samples:

Please join us
You are invited to a Mother Blessing for Donna and her baby.
We will offer Donna our support and love by making her a birthing necklace so please bring a special bead (that fits on the enclosed cord) along with a blessing for her as she prepares to give birth.
We have a book you can write in or glue in your blessing card.
We will meet at Donna's house, 12 Blooming Lane on October 7, at 7 pm
Call Mia to RSVP at 111-2222

A Baby Blessing
Please join Donna and her baby in celebrating her journey to motherhood with a Blessingway. Our intention is to surround Donna and her child with our wishes for a safe and fulfilling birth as well as our blessings for a joyful life.
Please bring a potluck dish to share, a candle, and your written blessings. Your presence is the only gift Donna wants!
Call Mia if you have any questions at 111-2222
July 15th, 6 to 8 pm, at 12 Blooming Lane

Time of day, location, and length

Most women have their Blessingways in their own homes. The act of honoring and witnessing a women in her own environment, surrounded by the things, colors, and space that she has created, supports her upcoming role as a new mother in her home. In fact, it can be wonderful to acknowledge the beauty and comfort of her home, and recognize that she will soon inhabit it in her new role along with her baby.

Though it is customary to have Blessingways in your own home, it's not the right choice for everyone. Choose a place that is relatively free from distractions (such as roommates, other children, or noisy neighbors), has enough space for everyone to be in one room, and feels safe and comfortable.

For groups of six or less, plan on at least two hours to gather, do the Blessingway, and eat something together. Larger groups will need more time. This is one event that you don't want to make too short. If a meal is included, add an hour, or better yet, just give a start time.

Whenever I do a Blessingway ceremony, I remember that it takes time to make a journey into a ritual circle and back out into the world. In Australia and on Borneo, ceremonies can take days to complete. For instance, in order to attend a ceremony at a remote native longhouse in the Malaysian state of Sabah, it took the guest-of-honor, the symbolic Hornbill bird, two full days to travel upriver to the longhouse. Men, dressed in capes of clouded leopard furs, eagle feathers in headdresses, and pierced earlobes that swung on the shoulders, sang and chanted day and night. The journey was in real time, though the Hornbill was traveling in a different plane of reality. Some of the Australian Aboriginal people do this as well—singing each step of a journey taken by an animal or mythological figure.

Before guests arrive, be sure to:

- *Turn off the phone*
- *Check the thermostat or air conditioner*
- *Boil water for tea (or have ice ready)*
- *Set the music*
- *Have lighters near candles*
- *Fill foot bowl halfway with hot water (fill rest with warm water when ready to wash)*
- *Have tissues, towels, brushes, pins for hair, nail polish, lotion, etc., ready*

Although this type of ritual is outside our own cultural practices, we can honor the fact that pregnant women do experience time and space differently as they walk between two worlds. As we plan our own Blessingways, we understand that the more time we can give the ceremony, the better. We can enter the transitional world of the mother-to-be by allowing lots of time to explore, release, celebrate, and fill ourselves.

When during pregnancy

Blessingways are most poignant in the third trimester. In the first trimester, a woman is adjusting to the physical aspects

Beautify your home so that the first things your baby sees are beautiful.

New adopters should give themselves a few weeks to adjust and bond before they plan their Blessingway. Whether they adopted an infant or a toddler, the new parents need time to learn how to care for their child without adding the stress of planning a big event.

of pregnancy, and the ideas of birth and motherhood are still abstract. There is also a higher risk of miscarriage at this time.

During the second trimester, most women are finally feeling the baby move and enjoying the pregnancy, but birth still seems a long way off. In the later part of the third trimester, women focus on the birth in a very real way and are trying to prepare themselves for motherhood.

The best window for planning a Mother Blessing is between thirty-five and thirty-eight weeks gestation. Some babies arrive early, and the last few weeks of pregnancy are often an inward time for a woman as she readies herself for birth. She may also be too uncomfortable to enjoy herself.

Environment: decorations, scents

Shelly kept dreaming of tropical islands and lush green jungles during her second pregnancy. She asked her friend Liz to help her create a mini-oasis in her bedroom for both her planned homebirth and her Blessingway. When Shelly invited her four closest friends to her small Mother Blessing ceremony, she asked them to bring potted plants (some were only loaned), green and blue fabrics and scarves, and other objects to turn Shelly's room into a jungle. While the hot July days steamed outside, the room fan blew the leaves and silk scarves like a tropical breeze. Shelly napped and dreamed in her private island getaway.

Not everyone wants a jungle in their bedroom, but listening to the dreams of a pregnant woman can provide inspiration for the decorations, music, and environment of her Mother Blessing.

The house should be clean, free of clutter, and aired out. A pregnant woman is very sensitive to external factors. Many will not like scented candles or aromatherapy oils. Others will want only one scent, such as lavender or rose, so check before filling the house with lilacs or cooking with vanilla or lemon.

A clean house can be a tangible reflection of the internal housekeeping pregnancy requires. Women who try to clean out their old habits, childhood wounds, and negative reactions have better birth experiences. According to research, women who are both physically and mentally healthy bond better with their babies, adjust better to motherhood, and are less likely to suffer from post-partum depression. It may seem a small thing to prepare a woman's home, especially if she is planning a hospital birth, but remember, her home is where she will truly become a mother. Encourage her and her partner to fix the broken step, oil the creaky front door, clean the refrigerator, and fill their home with beauty.

For the ceremony, choose a chair to decorate for the honoree. It can be as simple as draping a beautiful bedspread or tablecloth over her favorite chair. Maggie's friends wove streamers and flowers through a wooden rocking chair, and put a velvet cape on Maggie as she sat in her "throne".

Mothers, mothers-in-law, sisters, and daughters should be seated on either side of the pregnant woman. Make sure there is enough seating by adding floor cushions or even blankets to sit on.

Create some kind of centerpiece, also called a birth altar, for the middle of the circle. A small table can be used, or women often just put a colorful scarf on the floor with candles, fresh flowers, a blank birth journal, and other objects that represent the birth and mothering journey. Terry, who had her Blessingway in the redwood forest near her mountain home, asked her friends to being objects from nature that represented the qualities they wished for Terry to carry with her through birth. After the ceremony, she and her friends glued the objects together with a hot glue gun, creating a unique sculpture of driftwood, pinecones, a tiny nest, an egg-shaped stone, and buckeye seeds.

Lolo, like Shelly, felt drawn to water images and asked her friends to bring

Altar objects should include things that represent fertility, new life, sensuousness, womb life, and birth, such as:

- *Water, which supports your baby, in bowls or a small fountain*
- *Shells that mimic the shape of a woman's genitals and womb space*
- *Flowers, which open and unfold like a woman in birth*
- *Candles representing the light/life*
- *Berries or other seasonal foods for nature's nourishment*

objects representing the "womb" of earth, the ocean as Lolo thought of it. Her altar had a bowl of clear water, a large abalone shell filled with smaller shells, and a carving of a dolphin mother and baby. She added her favorite photo of her and her husband on the beach in Hawaii.

Sound, music, and movement

Sound is an integral part of a Blessingway. I say sound, rather than just music because sound has many forms, each offering a different gift.

There are many ways to use sound and music in a Blessingway ceremony. Playing cheerful background music as guests arrive helps create a festive mood. During the ceremony, music should only be used as a specific element of the ritual. At Tia's Blessingway, her friend Juanita played a voluptuous song to get everyone to dance and open her hips and pelvis. She wanted to encourage Tia to let go of her worries both physically and mentally.

Other sounds, such as a tabletop fountain, can be used, as well as drums or bells to signify the opening and closing of the ceremony. You don't have to be musical to hit a drum three times or ring a bell as a way to bring everyone to the circle.

To Angie, a singer and musician, music was very important. She asked each friend at her Mother Blessing to bring a song about what it means to be a mother. One friend made her a tape the next day. Angie loved playing the tape for her newborn son, especially after a whole day of feeding, changing, and burping. Each friend wrote down why she chose her song, which Angie included in her baby book.

Gifts

Shelly told her friend Liz that she didn't want any baby gifts for her Blessingway. "I'm so grateful for the support and I don't really need anything anyway," she said. Liz did tell the guests that if they wanted to do something, they could sign up to bring Shelly's family a meal after the baby was born.

Rachel was a young mother-to-be and had little money. She was glad to have her friends bring gifts, but many of them were also financially strapped, so her sister suggested that her friends give her hand-me-downs or shop in thrift stores for her baby. She ended up with a wonderful layette, and a few friends continued to look for larger baby sizes at yard sales as her infant grew.

The issue of bringing gifts for the mother-to-be needs to be decided on an individual basis. Buying tiny dresses or cute duck slippers is a pleasure for many women. If people want to give a gift, they will, and that's just fine. Family members and other friends who live out-of-town will most likely send gifts and cards when the baby is born.

Experienced moms know that the best gift is personal time and energy. Cooking and delivering meals, babysitting for older children, or offering to help with laundry, gardening, driving, or grocery shopping, gives the new mom a chance to rest and heal and just be with her newborn.

Many women who have a Blessingway request no gifts. Guests are asked to contribute something to the blessing—a candle, a dish or a bead, along with providing a meal later on. Babies grow out of cute clothes quickly, but a lovingly prepared meal fills much more than bellies.

If you decide gifts are part of your Blessingway, here are some ideas to make them more meaningful:

- ❖ Pool your money to buy bigger gifts such as
  - A roomy nightgown and matching robe
  - A day at the spa (to be used before baby comes)
  - A car seat (be aware that you need to know if it will fit in the car and include any features they want)
  - Baby carriers
- ❖ Bring gifts for the mom and not the baby such as theme baskets
  - Hair supplies, shampoos, and barrettes (personal hygiene will be challenging the first few weeks)
  - Bath salts, candles and loofahs
  - A date kit for when she's ready to reconnect with her partner (lotion or oil for a back or foot massage, a bottle of wine or sparkling juice, delectable treats such as strawberries or chocolate)
  - A facial kit with moisturizer, cleansers, face masks
  - New mom kit with nursing pads, feminine hygiene products,books
- ❖ Instead of baby outfits, shop for the things every baby needs including baby shampoo, soap, soft brush, nail files, spit-up cloths, socks, soft chewable toys, board books

- ❖ Film and a nice frame for the first pictures
- ❖ A baby book signed by all the Blessingway guests
- ❖ Coupons for mom and baby classes

MOTHER BLESSING PROGRAM

Every Mother Blessing is a unique event. When we honor the woman we know as she becomes a mother, we plan for:

- ❖ Welcoming
- ❖ Opening the ceremony
- ❖ Introductions
- ❖ Nurturing the mother
- ❖ Offering our blessings
- ❖ Creating a symbol
- ❖ Completion
- ❖ Feasting

Welcoming

Your friends have received their invitations, gathered their provisions, bathed and dressed for a party, and have now arrived. Like guests coming to a wedding, they are excited and curious. We do not enter a church talking on our cell phones or eating candy bars. This ceremony is just as sacred and special. Entering the home is the first step into a sacred circle. By signifying this with a simple ritual you are showing your guests that the ceremony has begun. You can do something as simple as putting a vase of flowers by the door, or you can welcome guests with rose water.

Hand washing: Julie greeted each woman that arrived for Shelley's afternoon Mother Blessing by silently pouring rose water into her hands as a symbolic purification and to prepare for the ceremony inside.

Simply add a handful of fresh rose petals to a bowl of fresh filtered or spring water. If it's cold, warm the water.

Removing shoes: This lovely Japanese custom represents the transition between inside and outside, and invites guests to relax inside the home.

Preparing a sacred entryway: Create a special environment in the entrance to the home with flowers, hanging fabric in the doorway, playing beautiful music, or putting a sign on the door saying welcome and please enter in silence.

Behaving like the honored guest you are means:
- *Arriving on time*
- *Turning off cell phones*
- *Bringing what you are asked*
- *Dressing appropriately*
- *Planning to stay for the duration*
- *Participating fully*

Opening the ceremony

It is important to begin a Mother Blessing mindfully in order to slow everyone down and ask them to be present for the event. Doing some kind of ritual gives everyone a chance to take a breath, let go of their own lives, and come together to consider and support the woman they are honoring. The more the participants can connect to their own feelings and thoughts, the deeper their capacity to connect and honor the mother-to-be. Everyone benefits from a ceremony. The nature of a ceremony is that it is a group experience, and so when everyone fully participates, everyone is nurtured and filled with the love and support they are offering.

Like every part of a Mother Blessing, there is no right way. Each circle of women will know which way works best for them. Chances are someone in your circle will have a drum, bell or song they can offer. Just ask before the Blessingway!

After everyone is comfortably seated in chairs or on cushions, one woman can signify the beginning of the ceremony by ringing a bell, hitting a drum three times, leading the others in a simple song, asking everyone to take three deep breaths and, in silence, lighting a candle in the center of the circle and asking for everyone's attention, or even doing a simple gesture such as a bow to the center of the circle.

❖ Instruments:
  - Bells, drums, Tibetan singing bowls, recorded music, or chimes can be played for just a few seconds as a sign the circle is open.

❖ Voice:
  - One person can lead the group with a sound such as "om" or a long deep breath with a strong exhale.

❖ Silence:

• A minute of silence is a lovely way to begin and no one has to say anything!

❖ Gesture:

• My book group begins and ends each meeting with a silent bow. We hold our hands, palms together, in front of us and bow forward from the waist. We've done it standing or sitting. Another gesture could be a yoga stretch such as reaching both arms overhead and then bending down to touch the floor.

❖ Lighting Candles:

• This is a very simple and easy way to begin, especially if no one in the room has done this kind of ceremony before. Say something such as "Thank you all for coming to celebrate and support our dear friend (name her). I light this candle in her honor."

❖ Prayer/Invocation/Evocation (see sample Mother Blessing programs, page 190):

❖ Purification:

• Hand-washing

• Smudging is a Native American rite used in many non-Native American sacred circles. Traditionally, one person lights a sage bundle and waves the smoke over each person to purify his or her energy. Pregnant women are often very sensitive to environmental factors so this may not be the best way to purify.

• Feather breath. You can simulate smudging without the smoke by using a large feather and wave it around each person.

Introductions

When we introduce ourselves, we are presenting our own history, lineage, experiences, ideas, thoughts, feelings, and beliefs. We begin as a circle of individuals, and through our introductions, sharing, blessings, singing, and celebrating, we become a community. Through the Mother Blessing ceremony, we are giving the space, time, and intention to remember that we are all part of something bigger than any of us alone. We get to feel our wholeness as people and to share who we are with our community. We may be gathered around one woman, but we all belong.

Honoring Our Lineage

Bonita Bliss, a good friend and the officiate at my wedding, started my first Mother Blessing by saying "You asked if I would share the story about when you lived in Santa Cruz, and next to your apartment was a huge redwood tree. A seed from the tree landed in a pot you had on your front steps and started to grow. At the time of your marriage, the tree was as old as your relationship and stood five feet tall. You and your friends took the tree to the forest and planted it in a cathedral of trees—its new community. You said the tree would always be a reminder of how love grows within community.

Calling on a Higher Power

A Blessingway, by nature, is a spiritual rather than religious ceremony. Because it is non-denominational, the language used is personal. Please call on whatever divine energy that is right for you. Invite and thank God, Goddess, Spirit, Higher self, Mother Earth, your ancestors, angels, animal totems, Divine Mother or Blessed Father. It is all good.

"Now, Anna, another 'seed' has landed in your 'pot.' It is a joy to know that you and Alex, as mother and father, will nurture your child with love and care, surround him with the loving protection of family and friends, and enable him to take his rightful place in his community.

"At your wedding, you acknowledged that you were bringing together two family traditions, two systems of roots, with the hope that a new family tree be strong and fruitful. So, as we sit here and look at your ripe full belly, we see the evidence of that 'new family tree.'

"I feel this is a great time to celebrate the lineage trees of your family and Alex's family, and to acknowledge your mother and Alex's mother who are here representing the family trees. Mothers, please tell us your names, your mother's names, and your children's names. As you speak the family names, we will invite them to be present with us in spirit for this occasion."

We went around the room: our grandmothers had names like Agnes, Violet, Rose, and Mary. Our mothers' names revealed the next generations of names such as Carol, Jean, Katherine, and Pamela. Then our children's names— Emily, Joshua, Madison, and Hannah. Saying the names out loud gave weight to our ancestors and to our offspring. It was a symphony of the past, the present, and the coming future.

Asking Questions

The question you choose can set a tone. Asking a light question such as, "what's your favorite flower" can make guests (especially those brand new to ceremonies) more comfortable. I've started my workshops by asking participants three questions:

1. Name a quality you sense from the environment (the whiteness of a lily, the smell of vanilla, the plane overhead).
2. Name a quality living inside you in this moment (my nose itches, my stomach is fluttering, my lips are dry).
3. Name a quality you are feeling emotionally (I am excited, I feel nervous, I am content).

You can ask any question of the group. Here are a few questions I've used to make introductions:

1. What is your favorite month, season, environment, scent, color, animal, bird, tree . . . the list is endless!
2. What have you always wanted to learn to do (play piano, bungee-jump, sing)?
3. What do you listen to in the car when you are alone?
4. What do you eat for breakfast?
5. What is one thing you love about the mother-to-be?

Stand Up If This Is True For You

This is a great way to make introductions if you have a large group. Start by standing in a circle. One person then asks a series of questions and if you answer yes, you step into the circle, then back before the next question. You can get started with these questions/statements and then add your own based on what you know about the group:

1. If you are a mother, please stand in the center of the circle.
2. If you are a grandmother . . .
3. If you have a sister . . .
4. If you are older than (pick an age just a little older than the youngest guest), then go up in five or ten year increments until the oldest person is standing in the circle.

5. If you're married . . . then stay in the circle; if you've been married more than five years, ten years, fifteen years, and on until the longest married person is standing in the circle.
6. If you have a job/career you love . . .
7. If you volunteer in your community . . .
8. If you work with children . . .
9. If you love to sing or dance or paint or ski or whatever . . .
10. If you have attended a Blessingway ceremony before . . .

Stories

Another way to make introductions is to go around the room and tell a short story of how you know the mother-to-be. For time's sake, I recommend doing this while you are grooming and nurturing her.

Nurturing the Mother

Everybody revels in the touch of another. Mammals both big and small snuggle, lick, and lean on one another. All mammalian infants require the touch of another mammal to grow well. Even before we get to see our babies, we eagerly anticipate caressing, holding, and drinking in the feel, smell, sight and, most of all, touch, of our children. To help prepare our friend or family member to nurture her own child, we can offer our own nurturing through intimate and appropriate touch.

Women sigh with satisfaction as we tilt our heads into the beautician basin to have our hair washed. We bring our best friends with us to get manicures. We hire trained hands to massage our knots away and to luxuriate in sensual touch. Nurturing the mother-to-be with loving touch can allow her to relax into her pregnancy, develop trust in her body, and enjoy the fullness of her soft, curvy shape.

Ask the mom if she is comfortable with these activities, but do encourage her to allow at least one. Hand massages are a great introduction. Once she realizes how wonderful it feels, you can ask if you can massage her feet and /or shoulders.

Primitologist Dr. Bill Sellers writes that grooming each other is, "the cement that keeps the primate social structure together. Gorillas and other primates establish and reinforce community bonds by grooming one another."

- **Washing feet**: Prepare a large bowl of warm water, have towels laid out and any scents the mother-to-be wants. If her mother and/or grandmother are present, wash their feet first. It's a lovely symbol of respect for our mothers who gave birth to us, and it acknowledges our beautiful lineage. If they don't want to have their feet touched, try gently massaging their hands with lotion, and thank their hands for all the diaper changing, feeding, caressing, dressing, and wiping tears and spaghetti sauce they have done (and will get to do again when their grandchild is born).
- **Painting toenails**: Bring a few colors of nail polish and cotton balls for between her toes. Wash her feet first if she is comfortable with that, massage them as you dry them with the towel and take your time painting. My sister Sue recommends putting on a topcoat as well, as it may be weeks before she can reach them to remove the paint.
- **Preparing hair**: Brush hair, create a new hairstyle, make a flower wreath.
- **Doing massage**: Gently rub feet and calves, hands and arms, neck and shoulders.
- **Making a drink**: Prepare tea or water for her to sip on.
- **Preparing clothing**: Ask the honoree if she has something special from her mother or grandmother that symbolizes becoming a mother to her, such as a scarf, shawl, cape, belt, hat or pin. A friend can also bring or buy something.
- **Creating a throne**: Many years ago I went to a bridal Blessingway and we decorated the bride's chair with ribbons, silk scarves, and flowers before she arrived. Creating a place of honor for her helped set a tone of reverence and delight. The chair was both a throne and a place of joy.

Offering your blessings

When you enter the room, you bring a self—full of blessings. You might offer your blessing by taking on a small job such as arranging the flowers in a vase that the other women brought. You might volunteer to brush your friend's hair and give her a new hairstyle. You offer your blessing when you sit quietly in the circle of support. You will share your blessing through your touch, your creativity, your voice, and your love. Every part of the Mother Blessing ceremony is a sacred act. You might see it as a divine gathering. Or an organic poem. You might call it a divine ritual, a prayer, or a gathering of gratitude.

What you bring, what you eat, what you say, what you do, are all aspects of the blessings you offer to your friend and your community.

Cradling is an activity typically used to build trust. Here it symbolizes that though a pregnant women is entering a rite-of-passage that she must journey alone, her circle of friends supports her. Though she may not know where she is going as she enters birth and motherhood, she has a web of women to hold her. Ask the honoree to lie down or sit in the center of the circle. You can hold her simply by laying on your hands as you gather around her, or you can have her lie on top of your outstretched hands. You could lift her a few inches off the ground so she can truly feel you holding her.

In addition to the many examples and ideas I offer throughout this book, here are a few more ways you can offer your blessings:

❖ bring something to place on the Mother Altar;

❖ offer to bring food, flowers or other supplies;

❖ offer to do something for the mother after her baby is born (cook, clean, walk the dog, take an older child to the park, grocery shop);

Symbolism of nurturing

Hair: *Our hairstyles reflect our place in our culture. Allowing it to be free is a practice of letting go as you journey into a new role. Tying it up or cutting it into a new style can represent your new role as a mother.*

Hands and Arms: *Your hands and arms will cradle your baby, and they will clean, cook, drive, wipe, brush, bathe, fix, and write, along with a zillion other tasks. Take time to soothe your working hands with lotion now so it will be a habit when just remembering to brush your teeth will be Herculean activity.*

Shoulders and Neck: *You may have the whole world in your hands, but you'll feel it in your neck and shoulders. Practice dropping your shoulder with a deep breath.*

Feet: *Treat your feet well—you will be standing on your own two feet as a mother very soon!*

Should you take pictures?
Taking pictures during an intimate ceremony can feel invasive. It requires a sensitive approach and clear parameters. One person should be in charge of photos. There are times when they should not be holding a camera, such as when people are sharing personal stories. However, taking pictures during the feast, and documenting the altar, environment, and projects is a wonderful way to capture elements of the ceremony.

❖ be prepared for the ceremony by having written down your blessings and brought whatever was asked of you.

Creating a Symbol

Making a creative symbol is a synergistic activity. The thing you create is a sum of all of you. It is bigger than any one person. It is a union between your humanity and the future. The void of the intangible qualities of becoming a mother takes form. The symbol represents the past, the present, and the future.

It is my hope that you are finding this book to be a symbol itself, honoring all women as we become mothers. I have also written a section with ideas for creative projects, including instructions, supply lists, and variations. Though Birth Beads are often the symbol of choice, there are no limits on what you might choose to do for your friend. You could make a mobile, a birth doll, a quilt, a collage, or a clay sculpture. You could also plant a tree or a flower garden; make a picture tree or a string of flags. Whatever you make together will be infused with all the qualities you offer your friend.

Completion

"Deep inside of every human being is this feeling that nothing is ever going to be complete, that the circle will never connect—and that itself is the secret to infinity."
-Peter Townshend

The ceremony comes to completion when you have created a safe, supportive container, filled with love and honor, and created something together symbolizing your blessings. It is important to make a final acknowledgment of the work you have done together. If you opened the ceremony with a bell, drum or chant, you can repeat it now. You can simply state your gratitude with a prayer or statement.

One of my favorite ways to open back up to the world after a ceremony is to hold hands (right hand palm down, left palm up as a symbol of giving and receiving), and do a "Sing, Sigh, Ha". To sing, take a deep breath and on the exhale, hold a note such as "Ohm" for as long as you exhale. Take another deep breath and then exhale in a long sigh. Lastly, take a breath, the next exhale with a sharp, quick "Ha" (much like a karate yell). You can send a hand squeeze around the circle by having one person squeeze the hand of the person on her right or left, and then that person squeezes the person next to her until it comes back to the original person.

Feasting

Before eating, always take time to thank the food.
-Arapaho Proverb

Part of every gathering is eating together, and Blessingways are no exception. Sharing food satisfies a deep need to nourish and nurture one another. It is also a familiar way to engage with others.

It's easiest to start with what not to serve at a pregnant woman's Blessingway: alcohol, coffee, or whatever food she may have an aversion or allergy to. When I was pregnant with my second son I had gestational diabetes, so the request at my Blessingway was for foods of color. I couldn't eat anything sweet or starchy, any white foods. We ate a lot of vegetables, beans, meat, and dairy that night! But since I had been on such a restricted diet I was deeply grateful to have my friends cook for me, and for us to share it together. I didn't feel so alone in my potentially dangerous (mainly for my unborn son) condition.

Jessica's mother loved to cook, so she made several teacakes and cucumber sandwiches for her daughter's summer afternoon Blessingway. They served juice and sparkling water—it was too hot for tea.

Miranda covered her backyard picnic table with all sorts of salads, fruit, and vegetable platters. She had cold shrimp, hummus and crackers, and a variety of cheeses. Miranda provided everything. It was important to her to give something

"Ponder well on this point: The pleasant hours of our life are all connected by a more or less tangible link, with some memory of the table."
-Charles Pierre Monselet

back to her friends who had been so supportive of her during her struggle with infertility. It was her way of thanking them.

Heather had her second Blessingway in the evening after dinner, and served tea and cake after the ceremony. She wanted her friends who worked during the day to feel they didn't have to rush to attend her Blessingway.

Ted and Fiona asked everyone to bring a side dish to their couple's Blessingway, and they provided meats for the grill, drinks, and dessert. They wanted to be sure to have time to socialize, so they made the food a bigger part of the day.

Another approach is to make the food a deeper symbol of the Blessingway by asking guests to bring food that holds some quality they want to offer the honoree. The guests can share why they chose the food they brought. Some traditional foods include:

❖ **Eggs** (deviled or salad) to symbolize fertility. Some Chinese parents hold a "red egg and ginger party," where they pass out hardboiled eggs to announce their child's birth.

❖ **Melons** embody the round, full, sensuousness of a pregnant woman's body.

❖ **Red fruits**, such as raspberries, strawberries, or cherries symbolize the passion, romance, desire and love that brought the child into your life.

❖ **Bread**, such as challah, used in the Jewish celebration of Rosh Hashanah, signifies the continuity of life—especially if it is baked in a spiral shape rather than the traditional braid. Breaking bread is a community tradition shared all over the world.

❖ **Noodles** are a symbol of longevity in Chinese culture. Long, unbroken noodles are used in most Chinese celebrations including birthday parties.

❖ **Sweets** represent pleasure, joy, and wishes for a sweet life!

Most hosts provide some finger foods, but others only offer cake and tea. If you want to keep it simple, just offer:

❖ **Drinks** (juice, teas, water)

❖ **Finger foods** (veggies and dip, cheese and crackers, chips and salsa, popcorn, olives, pickles, etc.)

❖ **Cake**

You will know what kind of menu to consider when you talk to the pregnant woman or adopting parents. What time of year and what time of day are important factors—although it can be fun to do a luau theme in January—but be careful not to make the food become the focal point. A Mother Blessing is meant as a time to be very present with your community, and to create an environment where people feel safe and comfortable to share their heartfelt blessings, and to build a cocoon of love and support around the mother-or parent-to-be.

If the Mother Blessing is at the mother-to-be's home, plan on having the Hearth-Tender arrive early enough to set out glasses, mugs, utensils, plates, and napkins. She should also plan to clean up afterwards.

Once you know your menu or potluck theme, ask guests to bring food that is already cooked and ready to go, along with their own serving utensils. Some microwaving is fine to reheat hot dishes—just make sure the honoree has a microwave. Otherwise, bring hot food in crockpots or in insulated bags to keep it warm. It is very distracting (and potentially very time consuming) to have women start cooking when it's time to feast. Be prepared!

Sample menus

Summer Afternoon Blessingway

- ❖ Cold drinks and ice (juice, water, sparkling water, ice tea, lemonade)
- ❖ Veggies and ranch dip
- ❖ Chips and guacamole
- ❖ Cream cheese and cucumber finger sandwiches
- ❖ Cheese tray
- ❖ Melon balls
- ❖ Seasonal fruits such as grapes and strawberries
- ❖ Cheese cake with raspberry topping
- ❖ Chocolate cake

Fall Dinner

- ❖ Warm drinks such as tea or cider, plus water and some juice
- ❖ Appetizers such as cheese and crackers, veggies and dip, and popcorn

Entrée

1. Lasagna or meatballs and penne, green salad and two kinds of dressing, garlic bread

2. Make-your own tacos with meat filling, refried beans, shredded cheese, lettuce, diced onions and tomatoes, sour cream, guacamole, salsa and chips

3. Hearty vegetable soup or stew, salad with two kinds of dressing, French bread and butter

Dessert—make one thing for everyone, such as a spice cake, chocolate mouse, a fruit torte, or a chocolate cake.

Winter Evening

❖ Warm drinks such as tea and cider, plus water

❖ Finger foods such as popcorn, banana, poppy seed, or corn breads, veggies and dip, spinach dip in bread bowl, hummus/baba ganoush and crackers, hot bean dip and chips, sliced cheese and apples

Dessert–offer a variety—homemade cookies, sweet breads, spice cake, truffles, and baked apples

Raspberry Tea

Many women swear that drinking raspberry tea in the third trimester helped strengthen their uterus and contributed to an easier birth. Some steep their raspberry leaf tea with nettles and add a little honey. It can also be made into an ice tea for summer moms. Try adding some mint or lemonade to iced raspberry tea.

II

PREGNANCY RITES AROUND THE WORLD

Rites to Remember

Nearly all cultures do the best they can to insure mom and baby are healthy. In many, rites are offered throughout pregnancy. These rituals support awareness for the pregnant woman, create a soothing and calm environment for her baby, and are tangible reminders of the essence of mothering. The Mother Blessing is the culmination of this sacred care. Some of these traditions can be incorporated into a modern Mother Blessing.

SKIN CARE

A pregnant woman's skin needs to be cared for, just like her baby's skin needs care after he or she is born. Not only is applying oil or lotion soothing and healing, especially for dry, cracked skin, it just plain feels good. Belly skin is not the only place where your skin is affected. Skin around your swelling ankles and feet, busy hands, tired legs, full breasts, and glowing faces also needs extra care during pregnancy.

When Nancy was pregnant, she and three of her friends found a private place in the redwoods near her home. She lay down naked on a soft blanket beneath the mighty trees while her friends respectfully massaged oil all over her body as they sang over her. She lay quietly for a few minutes after they were done, and thought about the fact that she was a creature of the earth and, like all creatures, she could give birth naturally. Her friends then made a wreath of flowers and pine boughs for her hair. Though it was a new experience for Nancy, across the globe, another woman in another country was also being anointed and honored in her pregnancy.

Rub lotion into your skin every day. Many women prefer little or no scent in their oils and lotions. But some like the gentle smells of lavender or rose.

MASSAGE

Morning sickness is over but now your low back hurts. Your legs ache. You notice your feet swelling. And the middle of your back feels stiff and sore. Welcome to the aches and pains of pregnancy.

As your belly grows and your center of gravity shifts, some muscles become over-stretched, some shortened, and some over-worked. A woman's body goes through tremendous changes during pregnancy.

In Japan, fathers give shiatsu (a type of Japanese massage) to their babies while they are in the womb. The father talks to the child as the baby responds to his touch and learns the sound of his voice.

Now imagine this: warm hands spread warm oil on your back, strong fingers knead into the pain along your spine. Skilled hands find all the tense spots in your hips and legs. Long hand-strokes go down your back and legs, reminding you of parts of your body you haven't seen in weeks. You breathe deeply, relaxing into the massage therapist's hands as she works out all the stress in your hands, your feet, and your neck. Your body sinks into the massage table as the discomfort of pregnancy melts away.

Massage during pregnancy is not self-indulgence. It is taking care of the unborn child. If mom's physiological and psychological needs are met, than she in turn can provide a more nurturing and healthy environment for her growing baby.

When you are pregnant, your body releases a hormone called relaxin, which softens all the ligaments in the body. Relaxin allows the pelvis to stretch, but all your joints are affected. Muscles tighten and grip to provide stability in the body. The result can be soreness and pain. Massage can help reduce and alleviate back and neck pain, improve circulation, reduce swelling, and alleviate stress on weight-bearing joints.

Massage also provides emotional support and physical nurturing. "It's a time when you can share your joys and fears with another woman," counsels Ruth Hartman, pre/ postnatal massage therapist and childbirth educator.

Perhaps more importantly, it can help you learn relaxation and breathing skills which will not only make you more comfortable in pregnancy, but also prepare you for birth. "The most important tool in labor," says Hartman, "is to relax and let your body do what it knows intuitively how to do. We need to get out of our own way and let it happen."

Massage and breath-work can teach your body how to relax, to go inward, to breath through contractions, and through the pain. It is a way to get in tune with your body. "The mother becomes more aware of where she holds tension in her body and learns how to let it go," says Hartman.

Massage is useful during labor as well. Most women prefer a firm, slow, and steady touch. Some women don't want to be touched at all, others only in early labor. And good touch for the mother translates into good touch for the baby. Reva Rubin, chairman of the Department of Obstetrical Nursing at the University of Pittsburgh, says, "Mothers who have appropriate and meaningful bodily touch during labor, delivery, or the postpartum period, use their own hands more effectively. This is true of both first-time mothers and mothers who have had more than one child." Touching your baby confidently and lovingly is a great start to a lifetime relationship. Start as soon as you know you are pregnant.

PERINEAL PREPARATION

At some point in pregnancy, every woman realizes the baby is going to have to come out of her womb. Then she realizes where it is expected to emerge, and suddenly the baby seems way too big to fit through her cervix. It seems impossible to imagine, and yet it happens every day.

One way a woman may literally warm up to the idea is to give herself (or ask her partner to help) a perineal massage to prepare the tissue for the incredible stretching act it is about to perform. The perineum is the muscle and tissue between the vagina and the anus. Many women feel that doing regular perineal massage, along with Kegel exercises, prevents the need for episiotomies. The best time for this massage is the very last part of your pregnancy and during labor if you can stand it.

You can prepare your perineum by applying a hot compress for a few minutes before doing the massage, but be careful not to overheat this sensitive area. After washing your hands, put some lubricant such as unscented massage oil on your fingertips.

If you are not comfortable doing both an inner and outer perineal massage, you can use an oil based lotion for the outside tissue. Please use a water-soluble lotion for inner massage so as not to irritate the skin.

To be effective, you have to really stretch the tissue, which means you have to press fairly hard. Your fingers and/or thumb should be about one to one and a half inches inside your vagina. Press down until it becomes a little uncomfortable but not painful. You may feel a stinging or burning sensation. Slowly, move your fingers along the sides of your vagina, staying clear of the urinary opening. Try to do it for a few minutes. The second day, you can rest for a minute and then repeat the process and slowly build up to about fifteen minutes of total time.

Do not do perineal massage if you have any kind of infection or irritation.

Kegels

Unlike perineal massage, which is a private exercise, Kegels can be done anytime and anywhere, since no one can tell what you are doing. Kegels are an exercise to strengthen the muscles in your pelvic floor. To do a Kegel, tighten the vaginal muscles and hold them for up to twenty seconds. Ideally, you should do at least twenty a day. It may be hard to do that many at first, so start with three sets a day of three Kegels in each set and slowly build up. It's always better to do one than none. Don't get caught up in the guilt of not having done all your Kegels. I found that one easy time to do them is when you're driving or talking on the phone. Do Kegels after birth to firm up the over-stretched tissue as well.

SCENTS/ AROMATHERAPY

Herbs are often used for both their pleasing scents as well as their therapeutic qualities. Washing women's hands or feet in rose water or brushing rosemary oil (for healthy hair and scalp) into their hair are common rituals in today's Mother Blessings. Lavender is a gentle stimulant. Chamomile is very relaxing. You can put a few drops of these essential oils into lotion or body oil or add them to your bath water. If you find one is particularly pleasing for you, put it in your birth bag.

Essential oils to avoid in pregnancy:

Basil	Marjoram	Pennyroyal
Cinnamon bark	Myrrh	Savory
Hyssop	Nutmeg	Thyme
Juniper	Oregano	

WATER RITES

The warm water envelops me like the water around the bab womb. Floating in a sea of safety and comfort, I feel like I am home a Home in a world of muted sounds and familiar sensations. I am movin through the water the same way I moved my first baby in this same warm pool during his first swim lessons. He, like I am now, like his brother who floats inside me, surrendered to this delicious feeling of trust.

I am being held, rocked, and massaged by integrative aquatic therapist and Watsu practitioner, David Sawyer. We are in a small shallow pool, heated to 95 degrees. He keeps my nose and mouth out of the water so I can breathe, as I am no longer the aquatic creature of my prenatal days. Watsu is a combination of massage and water therapy. Sawyer works extensively with pregnant women and their partners.

"Watsu helps moms and their babies have quality time and bonding," said Sawyer. "For dads, it's a way of bringing them into the birth process."

One father-to-be, after his first session with Sawyer, described his feelings of finally creating a relationship with his unborn child. He kinesthetically experienced the sensations of being in the womb. He felt himself moving away from the walls of the uterus to be born into air and light and sound. He said he had compassion for that journey his child must take, and that he felt much closer to his unborn child.

Being in the water is akin to a prenatal experience, making it very appropriate for pregnancy. Most people have an intellectual understanding of the mechanics of pregnancy and birth, but until it is experienced, it is usually only in our heads and not in our bodies. The irony, of course, is that pregnancy and birth require no thought, but only body knowledge and surrender to that natural, physical process.

Sawyer also works with women who are hoping to conceive. Often, he massages the forehead as the point of implantation. "The first cells that attach themselves to the wall of the uterus are the cells that form the front of the head," explained Sawyer. "Depending on the receptivity of the uterus, if it's hard or pliant, a person's psyche can be affected by that initial contact with another."

Images of implantation come up for a lot of his clients. Jody, one of Sawyers clients, saw herself as a strand of seaweed with an egg attached a giant egg, fertile and rich," she said. "I saw content in my womb. My first child had bro- a big soft feather bed, filling it with love."

lows the mom to be in the same medium as ne flow, the rhythms, the motions are reminis- nb in a fluid, organic way."

a natural outgrowth of the body-centered psy- the cticed. He found he was going back earlier and earlier in time wit ents around a variety of issues. "Watsu can help people go through a deep emotional process and let go of old traumas or issues," Sawyer explains. "The water then can support the person's healthy self-development."

Even for those women (and their partners) who aren't working through personal birth trauma or other issues, Watsu is a wonderful experience for pregnant women. Being held like a child and moved through the water is nurturing. The aches of pregnancy seem to wash away rather than be worked away as in a traditional massage. Suspended in fluid, like an amniotic bath, we can experience weightlessness and ease of motion.

I was reluctant to get out of the water. It was like leaving home. Lifting my legs up the pool steps was like walking through mud. I felt heavy again, a sea creature back on land. But soon, the weight lifted and I felt freedom in my spine and neck and openness in my heart. Although I was no longer in the water, I carried the memory and my own womb bath inside of me.

You don't have to do Watsu to benefit from being in water. Floating in a swimming pool can bring a deep sense of relaxation coupled with a delightful connection to your baby. Ritual bathing is done all over the world. Southwest Native Americans used the suds from the yucca plant. The Sudanese rub a nourishing herbal porridge on the mother. And other rites-of-passage, such as baptisms, are symbolized by immersion in water.

Dark, unknowable, and mysterious, the ocean is much like a woman's womb. Water represents the life-force in all agricultural societies. Without water, there is no food. And without women bearing children, there is no human life.

Water is also a potent symbol for birth. I dreamed I was a sea otter giving birth to my third child, who indeed slipped out after only an hour of labor. Some Native American mothers use herbs, both to wash with as well as to drink, that have liquid qualities such as slippery elm bark. Raspberry leaf tea is commonly used by modern women to prepare the uterus for birth. I drank many cups of it in my first pregnancy and my labor was only three hours. I couldn't stand to drink it during my second pregnancy and it took more than twice as long to give birth to my middle child.

Many women are drawn to water and water images during pregnancy. The element of water is appropriate in any Blessingway. It can be symbolized by a bowl of water on the mother altar, or by having guests ritually wash their hands in rose water before entering the ceremony. Washing the pregnant women's feet is another thing you can do.

WEARING SYMBOLS

Tying on charms, bracelets, or amulets during pregnancy is another worldwide symbol. The Sudanese women tie a bracelet on a woman near her birth time, as well as a thong around her waist. In Hellenistic Egypt, pregnant women wore rings that showed a womb stylized as an upside-down pot, with a toothed image next to the neck, which was the key to her womb. Thousands of years later, an early-modern Hebrew brooch continues this tradition. One side has a blue stone and the other contains a prayer, "O Gracious and merciful God, be gracious and merciful to this woman that she not abort and that the birthing come out at its appropriate time and be healthy."

Mayan women wore jewelry made of snail shells so that the baby's birth would be as slippery and easy as a snail coming out of its shell.

One of my favorite symbols to offer at a Mother Blessing is the ritual knotting of a pregnant women's community. Sarah, pregnant with her fourth baby, incorporated this ancient tradition in her intimate Mother Blessing. Sarah asked her five best friends to join her in her bedroom on a warm July afternoon.

Sarah slowly looked at each woman before she spoke, "I have asked you here because you are my closest friends. As you know, I'm a bit freaked about how I am going to be able to take care of four kids—three seem to be keeping me very busy. You are each inspiring to me as mothers. I was thinking about what I wanted to do today and I thought that I would ask you to tell me what you think is your best quality as a mother. Can you share one quality you have that makes you a good mother? I think I'm going to need what you have."

Sarah's friends were silent for a moment, each considering her answer. Tammy went first, "My sense of humor," she said. "It keeps me from pulling out my hair!"

Josie decides it's her flexibility. Jane says her best quality is her passion. Rose takes a deep breath and says it's her love. Sarah goes last, " I think mine is that I'm optimistic. I am usually able to see the good in my son and even in my husband." The circle of friends giggles at the irony of Sarah's answer. Their unquestioning trust in her ability to mother four children fills her heart.

As the women shared their qualities, they tied five strands, one for each woman, of colored wool yarn on their wrists. They knotted all five strands together and as each woman had her turn, she tied her section on her wrist with a knot. They had to sit close together as they were still connected through the yarn. Their qualities were now symbolically tied together and shared by all. They went around again with a pair of scissors and as they snipped their own bracelet off, they stated their quality along with their wishes for Sarah's experience of birth and motherhood.

The bracelets linked them to Sarah throughout the rest of her pregnancy and through the birth of her baby. Though twisted and frayed, all the women kept their bracelets on until Sarah's new daughter was a few weeks old.

Other charms:

Birthing Sachet: Some women like to make birthing sachets. They bless a handful of herbs and leaves, which can include willow, lavender, rose, and clove, and tie them into a small cloth or bag. The sachet can be used as an object of meditation, it can be worn, or it can go under the pregnant women's pillow. The color of the sachet can be considered as well.

Green: Healing, Intelligence

White: Purification, Innocence

Yellow: Joy, Playfulness
Orange: Creativity, Inspiration, Power
Purple: Spirituality, Intuition
Pink: Protection, Love
Red: Passion, Energy, Vitality
Blue: Calm, Serenity, Relaxation

Jewelry: Rings, bracelets, and necklaces are worn for many reasons. Tibetan women wear turquoise and coral, adding beads as they go through life. Amber is often worn by pregnant women as it represents holding life. Crystal hearts, silver goddess icons, or any symbol that speaks to the mother can be worn as a reminder of the sacredness of the journey she is on.

Joelle wore a ring with her child's expected birthstone in it for each of her pregnancies. She fiddled with it when she felt nervous or anxious. After her baby was born, she hung it on a ribbon near the changing table. Joelle planned to give the rings to the children when they were grown-up and ready to start their own families.

Grace's sister gave her a necklace of an archetypal goddess for her pregnancy. Grace wore it whenever she needed to remember how much she was loved and that she did have a community supporting her.

ATTITUDES AND AFFIRMATIONS

> *When a baby is still inside you, before you give birth, you have many thoughts. You think, 'The day I give birth, will I be courageous? Will I be afraid? Will I live? The day I feel the pains, will my heart be strong enough to withstand it?'*
>
> - Nisa, a !Kung Woman

Having a positive attitude towards pregnancy and birth is deliberately ritualized in many traditions. The Navajo people firmly believe in positive thinking. They show it through song and prayer as well as in physical ways, such as loosening a woman's hair, or making sure there are no obstacles in her way as she walks through contractions.

In the Italian Renaissance, pregnant women would meditate upon a special plate that bore the image of a cherubic St. John, holding a cross and heralding a banner. The intention was to use the image, complete with ripe figs and bursting pomegranates, to encourage a healthy pregnancy and to hope for a boy, also a symbol of strong fertility.

Chinese mothers-to-be take time out daily to meditate with their babies as a way to calm their minds and to start bonding with their babies. Thai people believe that their unborn children are affected by their mother's mental state, which has been proven by scientists to be true. A Thai mother makes sure her internal and external environments are happy and healthy.

Still, every woman has fears. For women like Nisa, who live in cultures where women, especially first-timers, do die in childbirth, it's understandable to be scared. But the culture also understands that a positive approach is a way to take action against fears.

What you can do?

Reframe and re-language your fears and anxieties

The two biggest fears pregnant women have are 1) is the baby healthy? and 2) can I handle the pain of birth? Fathers have a different fear—they fear losing their wives. It's important to recognize this difference. Women also have fears about being in the hospital, having to have an IV or a Cesarean section, hemorrhaging, or other complications. Every pregnant woman has worried for at least a minute about whether or not her baby is okay. It's a universal fear, and one that a Blessingway can help support. Since birth does ride the edge between life and death, it's very natural that a woman would have to face her fears as she waddles on the edge. Begin by considering what fears or anxieties you are ready to reframe into affirmations.

1. Are you afraid of the pain of birth? Try saying that you welcome the contractions that herald your baby's arrival.

2. Are you comfortable being pregnant? You could say how grateful you are to have a strong, beautiful body that is doing so well at providing for your child.

3. Are you concerned about the changes of becoming a mother? Reframe your fears by telling yourself that you are already a good mother, look how well your baby is doing.

Use affirmations

Write a sentence, on a post-it or small piece of paper, about what you want your pregnancy to be like and post it in your car, on your bathroom mirror, on the refrigerator, or anywhere else you will see it daily. Use one of these or write one of your own.

I am beautiful, calm, aware and relaxed
I birth easily and effortlessly
I feel strong, capable and comfortable
I am supported by the people who love me and my baby

Say or sing your affirmations. Saying them to yourself while looking in a mirror is a powerful way to teach yourself new ways of thinking. The more you squirm at the idea of talking to yourself in the mirror, the more it will help you. Throughout my first pregnancy, I listened to a tape of ocean sounds and talked to myself. I would breathe deeply, noticing all the sensations in my body—my squished bladder or my baby's heel poking me in the ribs—and I would tell myself to surrender to the process. I talked to my baby about how excited I was he was coming soon, and how much I trusted him to be birthed easily and effortlessly. When the day finally came and my contractions were coming fast, I paused for the minute I had between them to look at myself in the bathroom mirror. Out loud I said, "Okay Baby, this is it. We're going to birth you now. You tell me if there's anything I need to know. We'll do this together. Gently. Easily. I love you so much. I can't wait to meet you and hold you in my arms." Without thinking, since I had practiced it so often, I told myself "surrender" as I moved into transition, the most chaotic part of birth. My son's head started to emerge. Just when I thought I couldn't do it anymore I told myself again, "surrender," and the fear that was making me tight lost it's hold, and my sweet son slipped into the world.

Make an affirmation tape. You will need a blank audiocassette and tape recorder. The twelve-minute answering machine tapes work great, especially if you want to hear it over and over without having to rewind it. Use a separate microphone if possible. You can write out the script before you record it or just do it spontaneously. Play it at night while you are sleeping and watch how you change. Be sure to make yourself comfortable by lying on your side and supporting your legs and back with extra pillows.

To figure out what to say in your tape, choose the fear that you most want to overcome. If you don't, chances are good that it will find its way into your pregnancy or birth and sabotage your efforts. Free your mind and the rest will follow. Choose one fear or issue. The mind does best at relearning when you've chosen a clearly stated goal that is repeated many times.

Write and speak your affirmations into the audiocassette using the word "I," and a present-tense verb. Affirmations always are in present tense. It may not feel genuine at first, but it will. It's a little like smiling even when you don't really feel like it. Just the act makes a difference in your emotional state. Smile right now—you'll feel what I mean. It may be difficult to say the words the first time, especially if it's a deep fear or an old wound that you are reframing.

Here's a sample script for someone who wants to deal with her fears of not being able to handle the pain of birth.

Hello you beautiful pregnant woman. Are you ready to release and sink into your own skin? Take a nice deep breath and close your eyes. As you exhale, begin to allow each muscle in your body to relax. Feel yourself getting heavier with each breath. Feel the bed supporting all your weight. Feel the earth further below you and remember how easily and effortlessly she can support you.

Notice the rhythm of your relaxed breathing. Let any other sounds around you fade to the background so you can only hear your own breath and your own voice.

Now, starting with your face, allow all the tension to let go, gently and easily. Allow the muscles around your jaw and neck to relax as you sink deeper and deeper into total comfort where your body is lovingly supported and your breath is even and calm.

Imagine your eyelids feeling heavy now and your forehead softening, as you feel more and more relaxed. Allow the warmth of relaxation to go down your spine as each vertebra lets go. Imagine the warmth spreading down into your arms and all the way out to the tips of your fingers. Each exhale brings more and more relaxation. You may notice tingling or warmth in different places. That's perfectly fine.

As you exhale once again, relax your chest muscles and the muscles holding your baby. Your baby may be moving or resting. Notice what your baby is doing as you continue to relax, deeper and deeper. Exhale into your pelvic floor and allow those muscles to relax too.

You are feeling heavier and heavier. You feel very comfortable now, just being. Breathe the relaxing warmth down into your legs, knees, and feet so that every muscle in your body is completely relaxed and completely safe.

Imagine that in front of you is a path. Look around you and see where this path is—it could be near the beach or in the mountains, or perhaps it's a path you know. Feel the path beneath your feet. It is very inviting. Start to walk along this path—each step making you feel more and more relaxed. The path is taking you to a special place. You can imagine this special place. It is the most peaceful place in the world for you. You feel so good here, so strong and sure and incredibly relaxed. Feel yourself there with your baby. Both of you are peaceful and relaxed.

As you allow the peace to permeate every part of you, begin to imagine yourself giving birth. When you feel the first contractions, imagine yourself right here, in your special place. Allow the peace and relaxation to flow through you easily and effortlessly. Surrender to the peace. Let each breath bring more relaxation. Let the warmth soften your jaw muscles and neck muscles.

As labor goes on, the contractions get more intense. Your uterus is squeezing much harder as your baby slides down through the birth canal. Focus on your breath and your special place as the intensity builds. You are strong. You are relaxed. You can give birth easily. Surrender to the sensations. Work with them to birth your baby. Let the powerful contractions wash over you. Stay in your body, noticing as the energy moves through you. Relax your jaw muscles. Relax your face. Let your body sink into deep relaxation between each contraction. You are strong. You are relaxed. You can give birth easily. Surrender to this miraculous process.

Every time you listen to this tape, you will feel more and more relaxed and peaceful. You will feel an incredible sense of well-being. You will be able to relax deeper and deeper, and when it is time for your baby to be born, the feelings of relaxation and peace will get even stronger.

You can stop here if you are going to play this while you drift off to sleep. If you plan to use this in the day, then you will need to add this section, bringing you back to full consciousness.

Enjoy your special place and the deep sense of peace you are experiencing for another breath or two, then turn around and go back on the path. Each step back brings you closer to consciousness. You will come back feeling refreshed and alert and relaxed. Come all the way back now. Start to move your fingers and toes and when you are ready open your eyes. You feel great.

Caron Goode, author of *Nurture Your Child's Gift*, helps her pregnant clients by making affirmation tapes. "The best time to listen to your affirmations tape is at night when you are sleeping," she says. "Buy a flat pillow speaker from Radio Shack. Hook this up to your tape recorder. Turn the volume on very low, so it's just barely audible. You can listen to your tape while you are asleep, and your mind and body will get it. For busy, tired, pregnant women, this is an effective way to learn. You can replace words in affirmation with pictures or a story that illustrates your point. Speak to your baby; tell your story and your images to your child, and all benefit from the experience."

Give yourself time to relearn and reframe your fears. It may take a few weeks before you sense a change in yourself.

SINGING

> *There is a tribe in East Africa in which the art of true intimacy is fostered even before birth. In this tribe, the birth date of a child is not counted from the day of its physical birth, nor even the day of its conception as in other village cultures. For this tribe, the birth date comes the first time the child is a thought in its mother's mind. Aware of her intention to conceive a child with a particular father, the mother then goes off to sit alone under a tree. There she sits and listens until she can hear the song of the child that she hopes to conceive. Once she has heard it, she returns to her village and teaches it to the father so that they can sing it together as they make love, inviting the child to join them. After the child is conceived, she sings it to the baby in her womb. Then she teaches it to the old women and midwives of the village, so that throughout the labor and at the miraculous moment of birth itself, the child is greeted with its song. After the birth, all the villagers learn the song of their new member and sing it to the child when it falls or hurts itself. It is sung in times of triumph, or in rituals and initiations. This*

song becomes a part of the marriage ceremo[illegible] and at the end of life, his or her loved ones [illegible] deathbed and sing this song for the last time.

—Jack Kornfield, "Song of the Sp[illegible] *with Heart: A Guide Through the Perils and Promises of Spiritual Life*

What are you going to sing to your baby?

Most of us love to sing even when we can barely carry a tune. We si[illegible] privately in the car or in the shower. It's something we do instinctively, starting when we are very young. Babies in utero hear music and songs and, after they are born, show a preference for those familiar to them. So sing to your belly or your partner's belly—your baby is listening.

Danae Shanti, a professional voice coach and performer, feels that singing is a lot like giving birth. "I still experience that scary moment of delivery every time I open my mouth to sing," she said. "There's this wonderful, loving self inside trying to come out through song."

When my mother gave birth to me, she was told to keep quiet and be a good girl. I wonder how much harder that made her labor. In the births I have attended, including those of my own children, connecting to the animal sounds within made the births more powerful and more real. They also helped me cope with the pain. By sounding and breathing intentionally, the tightening that comes with fear and pain is reduced. Perhaps that helps women who have home births give birth without pain medication—they are comfortable enough in their homes to "sing" through their births.

Many religions use the voice to give prayers. Tibetan and Gregorian monks are two well-known groups. Other cultures, like the tribe in East Africa, sing to welcome a new child into their community.

For Shanti, singing, like birth, is a natural thing. But also like giving birth, not always easy to do. "I sing," she said. "I teach people to trust that they can sing. I give vocal coaching to singer hopefuls. They give birth to singers."

Singing and birth are related, as Shanti pointed out. "Trying to run from our dream to sing is like trying to run from birth. We've carried the seed to term. Our baby is coming and so is our song."

Can you imagine maternity wards bursting with song?

dreams, and of values. Altars ection between your heart's is a sacred space, made with point for you to contemplate, cally, altars have been in homes And though for many people the ot a requirement for creating and

iece of cloth, a candle, and a photo or on a dresser, or can have it's own table. He

Place: Some altars are me be private, but a family altar is a declaration of your new life as parents so it is fitting that it be in an area you see throughout your day. If you are trying to conceive, the bedroom is appropriate. If you already have children, the kitchen works well. Find a place where your altar will be safe and seen.

Base: Most people use a piece of cloth to create a base. You may have something you got on a trip, or some piece of silk that you love. Jessie used her grandmother's scarf—it reminded her of her own lineage. Angie has a large ceramic bowl with candleholders that her husband gave her after a trip to Germany.

Objects: Look around your home for objects that speak to you. Anything can be used including:

> **Pictures**: Find a picture of you as a child with your own family, use a baby photo, or a spiritual figure you admire.
>
> **Candles**: At least one candle should be on every altar as the lighting of it breathes intention into the altar.
>
> **Nature objects**: Whatever is meaningful to you—pinecones, leaves, shells, bird nests, driftwood, pebbles, gems, sage, sweet grass, etc.
>
> **Sculptures, objects, and artifacts**: This is personal. Find things you consider beautiful. What makes you think of being a mother or a father? What qualities do you want to cultivate and what kind of object best symbolizes that desire? What

qualities do you want to bring into your pregnancy and into childbirth?

Arrange and rearrange your objects until it pleases you. With your family gathered, light the candle and say out loud your vows to your unborn child, or to the child you want to come to you, or to the family you want to create. Denise Lim, author of *Altars*, writes, "The most effective altars are the ones that are used. Every time you use your altar in a ceremonial manner, the energy field around it is strengthened. This, in turn, magnifies and deepens your devotion, contemplation, prayer, or meditation time before your home shrine."

A family alter is an artistic three-dimensional representation of your inner values. It is family art that is constantly evolving. After your baby is born, you may want to change the altar to reflect the new being in your home. As your child gets older, he or she will also want to add things to the altar, making it a symbol of your family in all its seasons.

BUILDING A MOTHER NEST

A mother nest is similar to an altar except that you move it to wherever you give birth. It includes items for mother-comfort such as pillows, music, and clothing. Building a mother nest is a personal process. It requires paying attention to images and objects around you that remind you of the qualities and values you want to include in your pregnancy and childbirth.

The best time to build your nest is as you prepare for your Blessingway. Many women take parts of their altar, along with a T-shirt, their own pillow, and their favorite music, to their hospital births. Be aware though, that most hospitals will not allow you to light candles or incense. You can, of course, light them at home when you are in early labor.

Use your nest during pregnancy to imbue the objects you have chosen. Play the music you have selected for your pregnancy practice. Lie down where you can see your nest-altar and breathe deeply as you gently contemplate your pregnancy, the birth of your baby, and your own birth as a mother. Gretchen used just one CD for each of her births, as she wanted the hypnotic quality that happened when she repeated the same instrumental CD. Many women do not like any music during labor. If they do, it is usually a favorite piece of classical or new age music, something that has a dreamy quality that allows them to stay focused internally.

Here's a list to start you thinking about how to build your own nest.

- ❖ Photographs—of you, your family, your grandmother, or of nature images
- ❖ Art—the drawings you do of your birth dreams, other art that speaks to you
- ❖ Flowers, stones, object from nature
- ❖ Candles
- ❖ Blessingway projects
- ❖ Gifts from friends and family
- ❖ Pillows
- ❖ Your own clothes
- ❖ Music
- ❖ Aromatherapy, essential oils, scented candles

The women I've worked with have created a variety of mother nests. One woman dreamed of being like a dolphin and giving birth in the water. She created a nest-altar with pictures of the ocean, and a bowl of water, and found CD's with ocean and dolphin sounds.

Another woman, Corrine, added pictures of her ancestors. "I felt connected to all the women that had come before me," she explained. "I loved that I was an active part of my lineage. It was a trip to me to consider that the baby growing in me was once an egg in me when I was in my mother."

Sheryl asked her best friends, who were mothers already, to loan her an object that was meaningful to them. She used them to meditate when she was on bed rest during the last weeks of her pregnancy. Vicki packed her hospital bag with music, photos of her daughter and mother, a postcard with a picture of a red rose blooming and candles from her Blessingway. At the hospital, the doula put the objects on a silk scarf next to her bed and referred to them throughout the labor.

Cindy and her husband, Kent, loved being outdoors and were looking forward to sharing their love of the natural world with their child. When they went hiking together, they would talk to their baby in Cindy's womb. As they walked and talked, they gathered stones, leaves, pinecones, and other things and put them in a wicker basket that they brought with them to the hospital. "It was important to both of us," Kent said, "to share our love of the outdoors and to include it in the birth of our baby. We wanted it to be one of the first things she (their baby) saw."

Make your pregnancy or birth altar special for you. What do you love? What objects represent your deepest core beliefs? What objects touch your soul with care and joy? What soothes your soul and hugs your body? Gather them now, and put them in a special place for your baby's birth.

SEWING

> *Women's work is all details, a lot of small stitches put into life one at a time. Needles keep the hands busy while the heart stirs in its difficult sleep; they weave a hypnotic and deliberate calm. Women have always done these things, made scarves, gloves, headdresses, quivers, swaddling boards, vestments, moccasins, veils, christening gowns, beaded necklaces to rattle in the dance – inner turmoil brought to ground and herded into pattern.*
>
> *Women rein in their sorrows, their loneliness and denial, and make it into beautiful things bursting with erotic, joyful color, beautiful things not called art because they happen to be useful.*
>
> —Sallie Tisdale from *The Best Thing I Ever Tasted*

In American folklore, women quietly announced their pregnancies by knitting booties. Later, the women of the community sewed a quilt for the baby, each stitch a tangible symbol of their love and commitment to taking care of the new member of their community.

Michelle Klein in *A Time to be Born*, writes, "Sephardic Jews prepared baby clothes during the last two months of a woman's pregnancy; but there appears to be no record of a celebration or ceremony. In one account, women sewed the layette from old pieces of cloth, with the most effort put into the baby's bonnet, the only item that would be visible above layers of swaddling and blanketing. Women decorated the bonnet with colored ribbons and a little sprig of rue against the Evil Eye."

In other parts of the world, the grandmothers-to-be or the midwife sewed swaddling clothes out of used clothes.

One Mother Blessing project (described in Section Three), involving the ancient art of sewing, is to make a community quilt by painting quilt squares then sewing the pieces together. Making an infant gown, or a robe for the mother, is another lovely sewing project. Teresa, a midwife, embroidered simple designs on newborn snap T-shirts as a charming gift for her clients.

COMMUNITY

Whom we choose to gather with us for our Blessingway, and whom we choose to watch over us in the birth journey, and whom we sit with after our babies are born, are the people of our community. That's why we have to choose carefully. We don't belong to a tribe or a village where every person is connected to every other. Historically, pregnant women and new mothers were not left alone. They were lovingly and carefully cared for throughout their childbearing year. Unfortunately, in the U.S., most women are alone throughout pregnancy and new motherhood. Visits to the obstetrician may be very unsatisfying as the questions and thoughts that are burning inside seem inappropriate to share with the doctor. Midwives and doulas can serve as the village listener, and the Blessingway represents the whole village listening and supporting the pregnant woman.

In Guatemala, one person is chosen as the pregnant woman's guardian. She or he brings small gifts in daily visits. The mother-to-be is expected to share her problems so that they are not transferred to the baby. She also talks to her baby about her life, and takes baths with special herbs. The whole village makes sure that she has enough to eat so that both the mother and the baby are healthy.

It sounds lovely doesn't it? Though it is not part of our society, it's possible to create our own village by seeking out other pregnant women and new mothers, as well as people who can actively and compassionately honor and support us. Sharing your anxieties and your excitement help you feel like you're part of a bigger community. It also helps create a healthier environment for your baby. Research proves that a mother's stress levels and cortisone release adversely affect her unborn child. Cultivating a joyful attitude through building a supportive community is good for everybody.

Cynthia Morris, a creativity coach, relies on her creative ancestors when she is feeling fearful or unsure. Like pregnancy, a profoundly creative process, we can feel like we're stumbling around in the dark. Never having been on this particular journey before, everything is unknown; everything is new. Even though we have information about the process, we still have to find our own way without a map. Cynthia writes, "To work through this, I ask my clients to think of someone who is doing what they want to do. I call this conjuring up your creative ancestors. Holding others as role models for success can guide us through the dark places on our journeys."

Though you may be in awe of the mothers who have gone before you—perhaps you think they are stronger, braver, or more capable—they, too, went through their first pregnancy without a map. Hopefully, they didn't go through it alone and neither will you.

MOVEMENT/DANCE

> *The most basic fundamental tool of magic is the body. Everything felt, seen, or experienced on other planes can be translated though the body into the concrete, physical realm. We can know things through the body more completely; more truly than with the brain consciousness.*
>
> —Vicky Noble, *Shakti Woman*

Dance is part of our universal humanity. All cultures throughout time have used dance to express that humanity. In places like Bali and Haiti, dance is used to create trances that blur the lines between this world and the next. In Bhutan, dance is a form of ritualized prayer. In Italy, the Tarantula dance allows the dancer to connect with the divine.

"It seems to me that when it comes to things that are good for your body and your mind and your soul, dancing is right up there with prayer and laughter." -Peter Schickele, who had polio as a boy

Depicted in sculptures, carvings, paintings, and the earliest writings, dance represents spiritual self-expression in sacred rites and celebrations. In Crete, evidence of the dance dates back to 2000 B.C. The ancient Babylonians held festivals and hymns to the dancing goddess Ishtar. The goddess Bharait taught the union of dancing and singing in India. Historically, women have been the dancers and the symbols of dance throughout the world. Pregnant women are shown dancing on a fragment of a terra-cotta vessel from Iraq, dating to 3000 B.C. A literal symbol of fertility, pregnancy represents the mystery of life and the transformative powers of birth.

Called by different names in many cultures is the belly dance, a pelvis-centered dance that mimics the contractions of birth. Repetitive contraction and release of the abdominal and pelvic floor muscles strengthen the birth muscles, tone them after birth, and reconnect women with the depth of their own sensuality. As an example, in 1967, American dancer Varga Dinicu posed as a mute servant girl and witnessed a woman giving birth in a tent in Morocco. She reported that attendants formed a circle around the birth mother, singing softly and undulating their abdomens, then sharply pulling them in several times. Dinicu wrote, "The [pregnant woman] would get up and do the movement in place for a few minutes and then squat for a few minutes and bear down. She didn't seem particularly agitated or in any pain. The only sign of strain was the perspiration that soaked her hair and forehead. She stopped only for midday prayers."

Dance in all its forms continues as a practice for spiritual as well as physical preparation for childbirth. Whether in a shiny studio or in their living rooms, pregnant women who dance are deeply connected to the ancient mothers who moved to their own music of the womb.

I learned to dance to the five life rhythms, as originally defined by Gabrielle Roth, with my teacher Melissa Michaels when I was pregnant with my second son. I've been dancing ever since! I use movement as a doorway to safely explore and feel the inner landscape. Pregnancy is a totally unique physical experience, and many women benefit from using mindful movement for deeper understanding, which better prepares them for birth and motherhood.

First steps

To prepare to dance, choose music that reflects who you are and how you (or the group) want to move. Don't be afraid to try something new. Almost everyone dances. Children do it instinctively. Parents often swing with their newborns while crooning a rock ballad from their own youth. Even those who cannot walk or talk can usually dance and express their feelings.

Pregnant women should consider wearing a baby belt, (an elastic band worn around the lower abdomen that support ligaments) or wrap their bellies snugly with long scarves. Dancers should be barefoot. Not only is it safer, but it also allows you to feel the ground beneath you and strengthen your connection to the earth. Don't wear socks or slippers as it increases the probability of slipping or falling.

Dancing is wonderful addition to a Mother Blessing. It helps everyone be more present, and it's great fun to dance with your friends. Just one song is enough to put everyone into their bodies.

The following dances can be done alone or in the Mother Blessing. These prepare you for the stages of birth and for the rhythms of motherhood.

The balancing act

Music: Slow to medium beat – lots of instrumentals.

1. Joanne Shenandoah *Life Blood*
2. Sarah McLachlan *Mirrorball*
3. Loreena McKennitt *The Mask and the Mirror*
4. *Her Song: an anthology of women*
5. Putumayo *Instrumental Collection*

This is a warm-up dance that gives you a chance to reacquaint yourself with all your body parts, even the ones you can't see below your belly. Take a few deep breaths to begin. Bring your awareness inside; feel the air and your blood and your energy flowing through you. Keep your arms relaxed at your sides or wrapped around your belly. Focus on your feet. Notice the way they make contact with the floor or carpet. Is your big toe touching first? Can you feel your arch?

Allow your breath to begin from the floor and move up into your feet, letting the soles widen and relax. At the same time, imagine your breath in your mind's eye. Notice what color it is. With each intentional breath, allow the awareness to come into your calves, then your knees, then your thighs as you start to move rhythmically and easily to the music. Lift one leg, then the other. Stretch your calves. Explore the floor with the sides of your foot. Continue up into your pelvis; rotate your hips in small circles, then in big ones. Close your eyes and find the sensation of your cervix and perineum. This is the doorway for your baby to join in your life. Connect with your perineum and cervix and ask them to stay closed until the time is right.

Allow the music to move into your body and take the breath into your spine, undulating slowly as you find the spaces between the vertebrae. Breathe into your organs, opening up more space in your crowded torso. Notice what your baby is doing now. Sleeping? Dancing with you? Kicking for a faster tempo?

Keep sequencing your breathing into your shoulders, arms, and hands. Allow the energy to move all the way out your fingertips. Gently roll your neck, relax your jaw, your eyebrows, and your ears. You should now be moving in a conscious way with the music.

Next, start playing and improvising. Rock back and forth on your feet, then to the side. Notice when you start to feel out of balance. What happens when you raise your arms? Move your head? Lift one foot and lift your arms? Play with the sensations in your body and notice the emotions they elicit. Are you feeling light? Do you want to go to sleep and not face the feelings that may be rising?

When I practice "the balancing act" (as I do for much of my day as a mother), I realize there is never a time when I feel totally in balance. It reminds me of when my oldest son was learning how to stand. He cruised the furniture for several weeks, not daring to let go of it. Sometimes I could see his legs shaking from the effort.

Then he started standing in the middle of the yard, but he would hold on to the garden hose. I could see how the hose served as a prop. It gave him the confidence he needed. Then, one afternoon he stood up on the front walkway without the hose and took a step toward me.

Standing, which looks like a perfectly balanced position, is the beginning of controlled movement. Yet standing has no resting place; you must always make minute adjustments to keep your balance. That is true in mothering, too. You might yearn for the elusive fantasy that you can find a static place of balance. It doesn't exist. Through dancing the balancing act many times, I have learned that the constant adaptations hold the key to my sanity. Just as my body, mind, and soul had to yield to the different challenges of each birth experience, so do I have to continually make adjustments in parenting. Things both inside me

and outside of me chang
ers feel so exhausted—an

Womb dance

Music: Sensuous music t

1. Angelique Kidjo *Fifa*
2. Putumayo *Women of Spirit*
3. Capercaille *Beautiful Wastelan*
4. Peter Gabriel *So*
5. Santana *Sacred Fire*

This dance/exercise is a metaphor
ing. Begin with your breath and your fe
open and relaxed. The mouth is connecte ... gina and
cervix, so by practicing keeping your mout ... you're practicing
for birth. Keep your knees soft as well and ... firmly on the floor.

As you begin to be aware of your legs holding you upright, bring your focus to your pelvis. Gently rotate your hips in small circles. Staying aware of your breath and your feet, keeping your jaw soft, notice how your body feels (whether you are pregnant or not!). Play with your body. Your arms can become eagle wings and your hips a cascading waterfall. Who do you become when you have a new form?

As you move more deeply into your own inner world, as your body loosens and opens, notice if you're feeling comfortable in this rhythm. This is similar to early labor.

Some women remain in early labor for hours. The contractions are manageable and, in between them, women feel excited, competent, and capable. Early labor gently puts the mother-to-be in the moment; the focus is on birth, not the laundry, the dishes, or her guests.

This early focusing is also the state many women find themselves in during the first weeks of new motherhood. Being tuned into their babies and their own bodies as they respond with milk and loving arms, they don't think about the "to-do" list. Early labor is sweet; with focus, you can still feel like you're in control.

Sway and play with your body and your baby in this flowing dance. Practice staying connected to your breath, to your feet, and to your jaw. Remember this dance as you, too, move into labor.

a tribal beat that makes you want to move

r *the new pulse of world fusion*

Ascher

ckey Hart *Spirit into Sound, Superlingua*

4. Laura Love *Pangaea*

5. AfroCelt Sound System

This dance is a metaphor for active labor and transition. With this song, you learn to surrender to the hard contractions and the wild ride of birth.

The tempo of this song is fast and wild. You should only do this kind of dancing after you have had a warm up dance. The safest way to dance to it is to stay aware of your feet. Arms, shoulder, neck, and head should be relaxed. Dance as if you're a puppet who's controlled from the feet rather than the head. Stay grounded to the earth, breathe deeply, and allow the big waves of energy to wash over you without drowning in the song.

Emphasize your exhale; literally blow out the pain and hard work of this dance of active labor. Add a tribal beat and practice staying connected and whole without getting attached to the music. Play with your responses, slowing down your movements even as the music gets louder and faster. It's not easy to do this; staying centered while outside distractions tempt you is challenging. So is giving birth.

As you practice it in this moment, beautifully pregnant, notice how you handle the distractions. Are you irritated? Numb? Overwhelmed? While you are dancing, just pay attention. Don't analyze your thoughts yet. Simply practice embodiment through the dance.

Take a few minutes at the end to relax slowly, get a drink, and allow your breath to go back to normal. Relish your body and all it is doing, as you surrender to the movement and honor your body's deep wisdom and ageless beauty.

SUPERSTITIONS

Many cultures have superstitions related to pregnancy. Those with high infant mortality rates ritually avoid bringing attention to a pregnant woman for fear the gods might harm the fetus. There are far more rituals and ceremonies offered after the child is born and appears healthy.

Historically, the Jewish faith had no ceremonies for pregnant women. They feared the Evil Eye and thought that celebrating pregnancy was acting prideful and would invite harm. They often tried to keep the pregnancy a secret. Even today, many Jewish families do not buy or prepare anything for the baby until it is born.

The Thai people are also concerned with evil spirits and do not give gifts before the baby is born. Having children is very important and the evil spirits are thought to be childless, unmarried women, a tragedy in their culture.

Due to a different set of expectations and the fact that most mothers and babies survive childbirth in Western countries, we can afford to celebrate before the child is born.

PRECAUTIONS

Every culture has lists of things pregnant women must avoid. Though they may sound silly, many are based in good health practices. In counties with no refrigeration, avoiding meat is a good idea. The Jewish custom of not eating pork is originally based in concerns with meat spoiling. The Bariba tell pregnant women not to sleep on their backs. They say the reason is that the umbilical cord will wrap around the baby's neck. But doctors in our country recommend pregnant women not sleep on their backs because the blood flow to the baby can be hindered. Different reasons, same concern.

In Western cultures we tell mothers not to smoke, drink alcohol or coffee, to avoid toxic cleaning products, not to use aluminum cooking pots and pans, get x-rays, or dye their hair.

Though we may laugh at the idea of not eating hot food because it may scald the baby or not eating food stuck to the bottom of a pan because the placenta might stick, we have our own cultural myths. Ever hear of the myth that every woman craves ice cream and pickles in the middle of the night? Food precautions are part of every society. Philippine women eat a lot of eggs to ensure an easy birth and they eat a lot of bananas so their baby has a cool temperament. A Nepalese tribe believes that if a woman craves spicy food she's having a girl.

All of these rites and observances share a common intention for the health and happiness of pregnant women and their unborn babies. As communities, we know that every pregnant woman represents our own survival both as a species and as a culture. Creating a Mother Blessing is a natural event when seen as part of the community continuum of care for pregnant women. A Mother Blessing creates a container for a community's gratitude. It ritualizes the critical role that women offer their communities, both large and small. When we honor our pregnant friends with a Mother Blessing, we are helping them begin their mothering journey with a tangible form of support, love, and gratitude. As Karen said of the quilt her friends made her for her first pregnancy, "The quilt is really mine, not my son's, it reminds me that I can be the mother I want to be."

How we keep moms and babies happy is less important than that we do. If mama ain't happy, nobody's happy. So begin mothering by learning how to take care of yourself. Massage scented oil into your skin, dance with your feet and fingers, meditate on your family's altar, float in warm water, wear your favorite color and enjoy that pickle!

III

CREATING SYMBOLS: CREATIVE PROJECTS

The hands are connected to the hear,
soul. The hands will always take you h

—Sonja

When a circle of friends makes somethi are giving her a physical symbol of their blessi a woman can wear during labor are popular, and s can place in the baby's room, reminding the whol they all are. Wall hangings and sculptures can be co . the middle of the night when the new mom is up with the n .n. Quilts can provide warmth inside and out for baby or mom. Hanumade books can become family heirlooms.

Many of these projects use objects from nature. These elements remind us we are not in control. We use the term Mother Nature to describe a benevolent, gentle force. We forget that though she offers orchids, seashells, and amazing sunsets, she also brings hurricanes, earthquakes, droughts, and blizzards.

We do projects at Blessingways to discover our beliefs about ourselves. Our bodies, particularly our hands, do not possess the capacity to lie or deceive the way our minds do. We can say all the right things and not mean them, but we cannot make something with our hands without our bodies being present.

Use the following projects to spark your own imagination.

Necklaces

Although this is the most common project, it is also one of the most beautiful, and is easy to complete during the Mother Blessing. Many women wear their necklaces through labor and birth, drawing on the strength of their circle of friends.

A talisman is an object believed to bring good fortune or to keep its owner safe from harm. The term originates from Arabic and Greek words meaning to initiate into the mysteries.

Anne Nicholson Weber, from Illinois, made a necklace with her women friends for her second baby. "I hung the necklace above our bed for the rest of my pregnancy," she said, "and put it on when I was dilated to five centimeters. Within moments, hurricanes of ook my body, and our son appeared an almost miracu- minutes later. My husband suggested that we should rent y necklace as an alternative to pitocin."

Her necklace was not only an object "beautiful, weighty and sacred," but the fact that she and her friends made it in a Blessingway satisfied her craving for something more sustaining than a traditional baby shower.

Supplies

1. **Cord**: a three foot piece of black cord (double length if you are using knots as spacers), or jewelry wire.
2. **Clasp**: you can knot cord but will need a necklace clasp for jewelry wire. Prepare one end before the guests arrive.
3. **Beads**: Ask each woman to bring a bead that has significance for her. It can be from her own collections, made, or bought. Pieces of shell or other natural objects work well, too.
4. **Filler Beads**: If you are using wire, bring a packet of small filler beads to put between each bead gift. If you are using cord, you can tie a knot between each bead.
5. **Scissors**

BEFORE THE MOTHER BLESSING

Make sure the beads guests bring will fit on the wire or cord. The easiest way to do this is to buy the string or cord and enclose a small piece in each invitation so that as the women find or buy their special beads, they can be sure they will fit on the necklace. (Note: if the bead is too big or a charm, tie a piece of fishing line as a loop to hang it on the necklace.).

There are several ways to create the necklace. The beads can be put on as each woman gives her blessing and explains why she chose her bead. She can put one or two filler beads after her special bead. Occasionally, I have seen one woman make the necklace by carefully arranging each bead. The drawback is that the women do not get to symbolically tie in their blessings, and the reality is most mothers do not wear the necklace as jewelry. Most women do wear the necklace throughout the rest of their pregnancy and in birth. where its loving magic supports their labors. Afterwards, some women hang it high on the wall near where the child sleeps, or add

In some circles, a necklace is created with a bead for each child born into the community. It is presented to the mother-to-be to wear, meditate on, or hold during her own labor and birth and then she, too, will add a new bead for her baby and pass it on to the next woman.

it to an altar
wound around
branch that was pa
major life-passage, such
birth of my children, extens
career changes are represented w

As each woman adds her bless
to the string, she shares her thoughts, w
es, and love for the mother-to-be. At Tia's Mother Blessing her friend Cathy told her , "This is an old Tibetan bead. I chose it because it reminded me of our trip there together." Cathy strung the bead on the cord and knotted it, "My blessing for you is for compassion: for yourself as you go through this rite-of-passage and for your child who will need it in this world."

Tia's friend Kim strung on a blue bead from her own Blessingway necklace. Soraya added a Chinese bead that had "Health and Calmness" written on it. Ariana chose one that reminded her of how beautiful Tia looked in the full bloom of her pregnancy.

When all the woman had strung their blessing beads, Tia's best friend, Juanita, added several more that had been mailed by Tia's faraway friends and family. She gently tied the completed necklace around Tia's neck. She asked Tia not to speak yet, but just to take in the blessings she now wore.

I advise women to either ask each woman to write down her thoughts before the ceremony, or assign someone as the record-keeper and write down what everyone says. The pregnant woman needs to be in a receptive state to deeply accept her loved ones' blessings, and it is too hard to remember each word. The scribe should also record a description of the bead.

For a smaller circle, a bracelet can be made, but I have found the necklace, if made short enough, works better. Bracelets can interfere with chores or holding the baby. Necklaces won't get in the way during labor and birth, or bump the baby as she/he nestles in the mother's arms for the first time.

"Beauty is the love that we devote to an object."
– Paul Sérusier

ght to your environment cre-
yang symbol.
made using natural materials
an make the structure of a wall
arn, or fabric. The mother-to-be
ne already uses in her home. Kim
bright and wild paintings in her
r her Blessingway by shaping wire
and , from thick black wire. It made a
stunning focal n.

I found a piece of on a walk by the ocean while my baby was safe inside me. I hung different colored ribbons from it and asked my friends both near and far to make some kind of ornament that represented their blessings. Feathers, lace, crystals, small stuffed animals, and small clay objects now hang in a wonderful medley of blessings.

Supplies

Natural Mobile

1. **Base piece**: Find one piece of driftwood or an interesting stick at least an inch in diameter and eighteen-twenty-four inches long for a wall hanging. Get two or three thinner pieces for a mobile.
2. **Attaching**: Decide what to use for attaching the objects, such as ribbon, yarn, fishing line, or wire. Tie them on before the Blessingway, making sure each strand is at least eighteen inches long. You need enough length to tie on the objects. Feel free to tie on more strands than necessary to provide a backdrop on a wall hanging.
3. **Objects**: Ask guests to bring small ornaments that they make or find, that represent the qualities they wish for you or the qualities that symbolize what you mean to them. If you are

making a mobile, ask that they look for lightweight objects. Make sure there is a way to hang the object!

Ornaments, objects

Choosing what to bring is a fun process. The hostess should make sure the invitation explains the project and what guests need to consider when they are choosing.

❖ You could have a theme such as only materials found in nature. It could be made of small stuffed animals. You could make it using just feathers or just things from the sea or things from the kitchen.

❖ One family, expecting their third child, made a mobile of little toys. The other two kids and their cousins hung Lego's, a rattle, a pacifier, a toy airplane, Pokeman cards, a pine cone from the backyard, fall leaves, and a little doll. It was a charming way for them to welcome their new sibling.

❖ Try the Japanese custom of folding 100 paper cranes for good luck.

❖ Another idea is to have all the guests bring photos of themselves or pictures representing their blessings. You can glue them onto wooden shapes available from a crafts store, and decorate the other side with paint or glue-on fabric or handmade paper. They will need to dry before you hang them.

❖ Hangings can also be made of written blessings. You can cut hand-made paper or painted watercolor paper into shapes such as leaves, circles, stars, or abstract shapes. At the Blessingway, each guest can write down her blessing or just write one quality. I have a garland of hearts with the names of all my women friends and the quality I learned from them draped across my office. You could also paint a blessing.

Alternatives

1. **Wire**: Use wire, which comes in different colors, to form an object either at the Blessingway or before the Blessingway. Groups of fewer than six can usually complete a creative project during the Blessingway. It's also very traditional to sit in a circle and talk while you work with your hands.

2. **Clay**: Sculpey clay comes in a rainbow of colors. It hardens when baked in the oven for about twenty minutes. It's a good choice if you like clay but don't want the mess of pottery clay. Like the wire option, you can do it during the Blessingway or before—just keep the pieces small and make sure you put a hole in them so they can hang.

Making the wall-hanging

You can either hang the wood and ribbons low on a wall, down where you are sitting, or more appropriately, place them on a solid-colored cloth in the middle of the circle, and rotate the cloth to each women as she ties on her own piece. Ask each guest to write down what she brought to include in your Blessingway book.

Making the mobile

This is really a two-part project. It will take time to balance the objects on the wood or wire and keep them from slipping off. You could use a basket to hold the ornaments during the Blessingway, and have one friend work with you to put it together on another day.

Mother Books

Every Blessingway needs some way of recording of who said what to the honoree. It's too much for the pregnant women or new parents to try to take in everything and remember it all. The most basic thing is to have a blank book or journal to write in, or glue in cards, photos, and blessings. It's also the place for the mom to later write out the story of her baby's birth or adoption. It can become a baby book, but it can also be more of a record of the mother's birth as a mother.

The Circle of Hands project (described below) is one way to make the mother book the focal project. Each guest makes a handprint in the book and writes her blessing beside it.

You can start making a mother book anytime, even before you conceive!

LINEAGE

Sarah's mother, sister, niece, mothers from her neighborhood, and her good friends eagerly arrived for Sarah's Blessingway. Nearly twenty-five women filled Sarah's living room. As a way of introducing everyone, the hostess, Liz, asked each woman to state her name, her mother's name, and her children's names. Liz went first, "I am Liz, daughter of Jean, mother to Molly and Quinn."

As the woman went around the circle, they learned whose mother had died, who had children, and who had grandchildren. A few women had tears in their eyes.

Then Liz held an egg-shaped candle she brought for Sarah and said, "I light this for joy." Each woman in the room put her candle in one of the three big bowls full of sand in the middle of the room, and as she lit it, she said one quality she wished for Sarah and her baby. Then they all, from Sarah's young niece to her mother sitting beside her, took a moment in silence to offer all their blessings.

Since there were so many women present, they decided to ask only Sarah's family members to share their blessings aloud for Sarah. For all the other women present, Liz had cut up handmade paper into egg shapes and asked each woman to write down her blessing.

Sarah's sister went first. She offered Sarah a silver necklace of a totem woman giving birth, as she shared her unwavering faith in Sarah's ability to mother two children.

Sarah's eight-year-old niece, sitting at Sarah's feet, quietly shared her excitement to get a new cousin. She hugged her aunt and told her she loved her. Someone passed around a box of tissues.

Sarah's mother, deeply touched by the ceremony, took a deep breath and shared her own emotions as she briefly told the story of Sarah's birth and how she, too, wondered if she could love her second daughter as much as she loved her first. "Now I see the circle of life here in this room," she said. "I feel so much love for you, Sarah, and I am so proud of who you are. You are a wonderful mother and a beautiful daughter."

When she was ready, Sarah shared her own feelings. "I am so full of gratitude," she said, "I look around at all these amazing mothers and daughters and I feel so blessed to be in your company. You have so much to offer. I want to hold onto this feeling as I become a mother for the second time. I hope I can be the mother you see in me."

Liz closed the circle with an acknowledgment to all the mothers, grandmothers, and daughters who gathered in spirit and in flesh to celebrate Sarah and her growing family, and to offer their support and love. The women looked around the room at all the mothers and daughters and slowly stood, hugging and talking as they made their way into the next room to share carrot cake and iced tea.

After the Blessingway, Liz and Sarah glued each of the egg blessings into Sarah's mother book. She wrote her birth story in the book and added pictures from her Mother Blessings. Sarah plans to add cards from her daughter's first birthday, along with a letter describing her daughter each year.

Communication is a driving force of our humanity. We all want to find words to describe our experiences. Through journaling, writing prompts, or poetry, we allow the words to make sense of our thoughts and to give our feelings names. We might use metaphors such as imagining ourselves to be an animal or a type of weather or a place in nature. Sometimes we'll make poems. Sometimes our words turn into essays or songs, and often they become part of the legacy we build for our families.

Circle of Hands

Sandy and Miles had a couple's Blessingway. They felt that they both needed the support of their community to witness and honor them as they became parents. During the potluck dinner and social time, they asked each couple or friend to come upstairs to their baby's room. They had taped masking tape to create a border about ten inches from the ceiling all around the room. They had two trays of wall paint and a ladder. Each friend dipped a hand in the green or blue paint and made a hand print in the border. Then, with their hands still wet with paint, they made another print in a large scrapbook that Sandy and Miles took apart so that each page could dry. After washing their hands, they came back and wrote their blessing on the page with their handprint. Sandy and Mile's son slept in a room encircled by the hands of his loving community. And the new family had a book they would treasure forever.

You can make handprints just about anywhere. You can add grandparents and out-of-town friends and family when they come to meet the new baby.

Some more places for handprints:
Closet door
Dresser
Book shelves
An oversized t-shirt for mom
Sheets and pillowcases for the parents and the baby
A plain quilt
A heavy tablecloth or light cotton blanket that can be used as an outdoor baby blanket

Supplies

1. **Scrapbook or spiral-bound journal**: Scrapbooks come in a huge variety, thanks to the new interest in scrap-booking. The best kind to use for a hand book is one with heavy paper and a fastening that can be undone so that the pages can come apart. Spiral-bound journals work well if you expect to glue in cards and photos.
2. **Paint**: For furniture you can use acrylic paints found in craft stores or, if you want the prints all the same color, you can buy a quart from a paint store. Household paints are all non-toxic. Fabric paints are readily available, and regular acrylic paints also work well on fabric.
3. **Fabric**: Cotton-based fabrics take paint much better than synthetic fabrics. Wash, dry (and iron if necessary), before you apply paint.

Quilts

Sewing quilts is an American tradition for welcoming new babies into a community. Though you might have a group of friends that want to create a quilting bee and make a traditional heirloom, there are simpler ways of making beautiful quilts.

Kathy painted a mural in her nursery, and she painted her baby furniture. Because she valued homemade items, she wanted her friends to make a gift for her Mother Blessing. With her friend, Shauna, she planned out an easy quilt she then used as a decoration in her baby's room. Kathy chose a green background to match the room. For her

Blessingway, she and Shauna covered the dining room table and the kitchen counter with newspaper or plastic sheets. They laid out a rainbow of paint colors, big and small brushes, sponges, stencils, and stamps. Each woman had a square white piece of cloth. Kathy asked that everyone paint, write, or design his or her wish for her and her baby. The more artistic women painted scenes. One woman wrote a long letter on her square. Another painted a big spiral. Someone else drew the moon and stars. A few days later, Kathy and Shauna pinned the pieces together and quickly sewed them on Kathy's sewing machine. Her daughter is nine now and the quilt still hangs in her bedroom.

Supplies

1. **Fabric squares**: Plain white muslin or cotton squares work best. Polyester won't hold the paint as well. Cut the fabric into squares at least twelve inches across and up to eighteen inches long. You'll need at least nine squares to make a baby-sized quilt. If you have lots of friends who will be painting; you may want to consider doing a two-sided quilt.
2. **Paints**: Offer acrylic craft paints (available in small bottles in a huge range of colors) as well as paint pens for writing words.
3. **Brushes**: Different widths.
4. **Stamps or stencils**: One woman, concerned about people feeling intimidated to paint, offered stamps, but she found that it took away the personal touch. Remind your guests that you can always just write something and paint a simple border.

Hints

1. **Borders**: You will be sewing the squares so everyone needs to leave at least a one-inch border around their square.
2. **Background fabric**: There are two ways to choose your background fabric. The first is to buy the fabric you want to use as the backing and borders before everyone paints, and let them see it so they can match the colors. The other is to buy the fabric after the squares are painted and match the fabric to the squares. You may want to use a solid color fabric for the borders and a print fabric for the back.

Borrowing from an idea some mothers do when their kids leave the nest—they make a quilt out of their child's old t-shirts, baby clothes, and favorite blanket. You can do a similar project. Ask each guest to bring a piece of fabric (12 inches square or larger) that has significance to them, and sew your quilt from the patchwork of the past.

3. **Sewing**:

- Before you start sewing, lay out the squares with the border and arrange it to your liking.
- Use straight pins to fit all the pieces together.
- Sew it all together.
- Sew the back piece on, inside's out (leave one side open so you can turn it out the right way). If you choose to use a filling, sew that to the back before sewing the two sides together.
- If you expect to use the quilt as a wall hanging, it will be lighter and less bulky without filling.
- Accomplished sewers can add fancy stitching and designs. If that's not you, hand-stitch a tie at each corner of each square to finish off the quilt.

Mother's Dress

Not long ago, maternity clothes reflected society's view that pregnant women were passive, sweet icons, and not real, sweaty, intelligent women. It's a whole new wardrobe nowadays. Pregnant women no longer have to raid their husbands closet for baggy t-shirts. They can wear sexy red cocktail dresses, tailored suits, or funky bright print blouses. Anything goes.

This new liberality in pregnancy fashion means that making clothes for mothers-to-be is as open as your imagination.

Making clothes does not have to include sewing. Another way to look at it is that you are decorating clothes rather than making them (though that could be the perfect project for some people).

Shayna, a newly pregnant woman, loved to wear unique, fun clothes. She shopped at second hand stores and boutique shops. She was one of those women who could wear lime green and make it look fabulous. Her friends decided to comb the thrift stores and consignment shops for maternity and nursing clothes that they could decorate.

Dorrie found a two-layered cream-colored skirt. At Shayna's Blessingway, she painted the underskirt with watered down fabric paint. The blues, greens, and purples blended together to look like a watercolor wash. The skirt shimmered when Shayna wore it.

Another friend, Paula, found a pair of Capri-length maternity pants. She sewed on red fringe and glued a rhinestone flower on each leg. Shayna loved the clothes. To her, they represented not only that her friends really knew her, but also that she was going to be a fun mom!

Supplies

1. **Maternity** or nursing clothes, preferably in solid colors. Look at consignment shops and thrift stores. You can also use new clothes, but wash them before applying paint or decorations.
2. **Fabric paints** and brushes.
3. **Buttons**, ribbons, fringe, rhinestones, and other decorations meant to go on clothes.
4. **Fabric glue**, needles, and thread.

Alternatives

1. **Themes**: You can use a theme such as color, style, or decoration. Shayna's friends picked what they liked. You could have everyone decorate a dress or shirt or have everyone incorporate the mother's favorite color or use a common element such as a motif.
2. **Progressive sizes**: It took Dara years to conceive and when she did, she invited all the people who stood by her to a luncheon where she announced her pregnancy. Her best friend, Anisa, wanted to do something special for her friend, knowing how painful the years had been. She decorated three outfits plus a nursing shirt for Dara, one for each trimester. The first one was not actually a maternity dress but a simple shift, which she decorated with a spiral stamp. Each garment reflected something about how Dara was feeling—Anisa used yellows polka-dots on a pair of exercise shorts in the middle trimester for when Dara would be feeling strong and beautiful. Anisa found a dress she dyed in sea green and painted on a dolphin mother and baby

for the last trimester when the reality of becoming a mother was drawing near.

Shape of Things to Come: Clay Sculptures

The immediacy of clay can allow you to access deep thoughts and feelings within a very short space of time, often enabling you to go on to draw effective conclusions about yourself.

—Vicky Barber, *Explore Yourself Through Art*

Ginny's box arrived in the mail the day before Chandra's Mother Blessing. Chandra carefully opened her friend's box and found a clay sculpture of a mother holding her child up to the sky. The gesture of delight in the mother and child brought tears to her eyes. She knew she would remember that joyful offering when she became a mother. She could hardly wait for her Mother Blessing when all her friends would make their own clay sculptures for her and her baby.

Chandra's friends and family sat in a circle in her living room. Chandra's friend, Rosie, explained to the six women in the circle that Chandra wanted to make something three-dimensional that she could hold in her hand and feel the heft of her friends' love. She decided on small clay sculptures representing the qualities they wished for her as she became a mother.

Rosie handed each woman a handful of clay, and a piece of paper and pen. Then she asked everyone to close her eyes. "OK," she said. "Now that you are comfortable, become aware of your breathing. Notice how your breath moves through your body—is it constricted in your belly? Can you feel it in your throat or your toes? Take a few minutes to just watch yourself breathe from your inner eye as you hold the clay. Just find your natural breath without forcing anything. Keeping your eyes closed, begin to play with the clay and notice the qualities inherent in it. It is cool at first, notice how deliciously it warms up as you press and stretch it.

"As the clay becomes more pliable, allow yourself to dream into your own mother qualities, whether you have children or not. Ask yourself, *what qualities do I have that I would like to share with Chandra?* See what images come to you. Pictures or symbols may come into you head or they may come through your hands as they explore the clay. Make the first picture/symbol that arises. Take up to five minutes to make the shape of the attribute or quality you wish for Chandra. Put it in front of you, take a deep breath, and write out an explanation of what it is on the paper next to you. Also write down the feelings of holding the clay and your reaction to what you made. Please remember to date the entry."

After everyone briefly shares what she made, Rose continues.

"Now pick up the piece you made and close your eyes again. Take three deep breaths and allow your inhales to sink down your spine and into your belly. Notice how your breath moves through your body this second time. And again notice how the clay feels in your hands now that it has a shape."

"Take one more deep breath and on the exhale smash down the clay into a lump. How does it make you feel to squish something you made? Does it remind you of when you finally get the kitchen cleaned and mopped and then the kids come home from school with dirty shoes, throw down their backpacks, grab a bag of chips and talk to you while the crumbs make a yellow film on the still damp floor? How do we continue to clean and beautify our homes and lives in the midst of chaos? How do we become over and over again the proverbial phoenix rising out of the ashes?

"The clay holds some of the qualities that make it possible to wash the same dishes every day. Its multi-dimensions are flexible, pliable, solid, and renewable. Like the warm clay in our hands, we can soften our judgments and ideas. We can hold our values, ethics and beliefs even as we are stretched to meet our parenting demands. The lump in your hand does not lose anything even as you change its form again and again."

Rosie continued, "Let's get back to the squished clay in your hands. With your eyes still closed, and your breath even and natural, go deeper inside yourself and allow another image to arise that represents you as a mother. How does that quality connect to Chandra? What clay form symbolizes it? Again, take about five minutes to make your shape. And again, write down your reactions, your feelings, and explain your clay form."

Often the first shapes women make are universal archetypes such as a round, fertile mother goddess or hearts and arms. The second shape is much more personal and often much more simple with rougher edges. Multiple arms might appear, or holes in the heart, or animal totems. Images that come from your soul, no matter how artistically imperfect they may be, deserve a place on your mother or family alter.

After everyone shared the process and their shapes, Rosie put them in the oven to dry while they washed Chandra's feet, brushed her hair and massaged her neck and shoulders. They sang lullabies while they cared for Chandra.

They moved to the kitchen so they could work at a table as they painted their shapes. The women who were already mothers shared stories of the births of their children, and those not yet mothers talked about their own dreams.

Chandra put all the clay blessings on her birth altar and surrounded them with candles. She put their written notes and blessings in her mother book along with photos from that day. When she woke up in the middle of the night a month later with her first contractions, she lit the candles and held each shape, thinking of her friend and asking for the qualities they shared to carry her through her birth. She especially liked the little bird's nest with three eggs in it. Her friend Denise told her it represented calm acceptance for her mother-work. The bird did not question herself; she simply did the work and cared for her children. It was a reminder not to think too much, but to just be the mother she was becoming.

Supplies

1. **Clay**: You can use either Oven-craft clay such as Laguna, or polymer-based clay such as Sculpey colored modeling compound.
2. **Craft acrylic paints**.
3. **Clear IPN Coating** (Acrylic polyurethane finish).

Instructions

1. **Sculpey clay** is much less messy to use, though it also feels stiffer. It comes in a plethora of colors.
2. **Hardening**: Both kinds of clay can be baked in the oven to harden. Both can be painted with colorful acrylic paints.

Spray with a coating such as varathane to prevent paint from chipping.

Good Mother Collage

Gabriella wanted to do something significant for her Mother Blessing. As a visual artist she loved working with her hands, and many of her friends shared her passion. She also wanted to work collaboratively on a project. One of the things that impressed her most about being pregnant was the organic feeling of being able to work with her baby. Gabriella loved that her baby ate what she ate and responded to her hands and her moods. It was such a synergistic relationship that she wanted to make a symbol of it. She decided she wanted her Blessingway to be about the relationship between mother and child.

Gabriella asked her guests to bring images or items that spoke to them about what it means to be a good mother. She suggested pictures, photos, postcards, and magazine clippings, in additions to pieces of fabric, ribbons, and things from nature such as shells, moss, bark, and flowers.

She thought about her feelings about becoming a mother, and carefully collected things from her house and on her daily walk. When the afternoon of her Mother Blessing came, Gabriella had a large canvas ready along with acrylic paints, brushes, and aprons. Her basket of supplies was filled with her favorite tea, a picture of her mother and grandmother, a postcard of a giraffe with her baby, tiny pink shells, lichen and leaves from her walks, and a picture of herself, among other things.

She wrote in her mother book journal:

When I look inside to find the aspects of my internal good mother, I find myself. The resources she needs are what I need. I am often like a she-bear; I hide in the winter in the warmth and safety of my home, nurturing my cubs. I am devoted to my young and I can be quick with a paw cuff when they go astray. In the summer, I become a sea otter, rolling in the surf along the chilly Pacific waters, rich in kelp and plankton. I ride the waves of my womb, sharing my sea with seals and salmon, sharks and sea urchins. I eat abalone and crabs. And the bear in me seeks raspberries and tender greens. I like naps and floating in kelp beds and wildflower meadows. I like the sun against my skin and quiet. I am very happy when I am alone. I am always aware of the edges, where my body meets the air or the sea. It gives me grace. I pray in the temples of mother earth, in rocky outcroppings near the crashing surf, in muffled pine forests on south facing slopes.

Her friends had similar visions of what it means to be a good mother. They painted and glued images of trees, rooted and reaching. They used a lot of greens and blues to symbolize rivers of life. One friend added a fire coming out of a women's belly. Another put in a coat and shoes, metaphors for care-taking.

Gabriella swirled the loose tea into the paint. She painted a spiral around the pictures of herself, her mother, and her grandmother that she glued on the canvas. She typed up a poem she wrote and glued it in among the trees, rivers, and coats. After it dried, she framed it and hung it in her bedroom so she could draw strength from it every morning when she opened her eyes, and every night when she finally closed them. Her friends like to visit the Good Mother collage whenever they come over.

Here's the poem she wrote:

I am Mother
I am strong and fearless.
I hold the world in my belly. Giving birth to one child at a time,
to one story at a time.
I tell my sons that connection is more important than knowledge.
I tell my daughters that we must give each other what we need.
I am Mother.
I am resourceful and resourced.
I take deep breaths.
I tell my sons that only real men cry.
I tell my daughter that pink is the color of power.
I am Mother
Inside and outside
In the ocean of my womb,
In the fire of my cave.
I am Mother.

I tell my mate that his blue eyes focus the world for me.
I tell him that his hands hold the streams of real life.
I tell him that he moves like a god, full of vision and discernment.
I am Mother and I am her child.
I tell her that I am afraid she will leave me.
And I know that I will be the one to leave, as it has always been.
I am my mother's child, a mother of children.
I know this: without a good sense of the healthy mother,
 it is impossible to experience abundance. (1999)

Supplies

1. **Canvas**: Stretched artist canvas at least 18" by 18". The bigger it is, the more everyone can contribute. You can get these at most art supply stores.
2. **Acrylic paints**: Choose your favorite colors. Acrylic will not wash out of clothes so make sure you have aprons or have guests wear painting clothes
3. **Brushes**: Supply several brushes in different widths.
4. **Collage materials**: photos, magazines, cards, shells, tea, etc. Anything that can be easily glued on will work.
5. **Words**: Gabriella typed up her poem before the Mother Blessing so it would be ready. You can also write on handmade paper or cut words from magazines.

Through Gabriella's story, you can see there are many ways to make a good mother collage. If you wanted something with a certain theme or color range, make that clear to your guests. For example, you could make it all sea and water images or pictures of mothers.

Containing Yourself

MOTHER BOXES OR BLESSING BASKETS

Eliza was a kaleidoscope of emotions. One minute she felt thrilled to be pregnant again and incredibly blessed. The next she felt totally overwhelmed with her life. She already had two kids, her marriage was on the rocks, and she could barely manage to keep the housework up.

Eliza didn't ask her friends for a Blessingway because she didn't feel worthy of the attention.

Her friend Fiona set one up anyway. She talked to Eliza about what she needed. Eliza told her, " I feel like I'm barely holding on here and I can't keep it together. I need something to keep me from falling apart."

Fiona listened quietly and then she said, "It sounds like you need some kind of container to hold your life together. We can do that for you—we can make a container and fill it will all the things you need. We could put in comfort, rest, joy, clarity, strength, and more. How does that sound?"

Here is what Eliza's friends put in her basket:

❖ Raw white wool for soft warmth

❖ Leather cord for strength

❖ A handful of pennies for abundance and awareness. Her friend Andrea has a sacred money pile—she told them she finds coins almost every day.

❖ Worry dolls

❖ A fabric turtle for the soft part that must come forward if the turtle wants to move at all

❖ A red ribbon with the words Ask – Listen – Receive – Open –Forgive – Ask, written from end to end

❖ Beeswax candles that her friend had made with her son. She said her blessing was about connecting with her loved ones

❖ Two open hands and long arms that wrapped around the whole basket to remind Eliza that she can hold the whole world and to let it hold her

❖ Turquoise beads that had been a gift to her friend

You can decide to have the mother-to-be create the container before the Mother Blessing, or you can have her buy a container such as a basket. Baskets with wire sides work well if you plan to weave in ribbons or cloth.

In the invitation, ask each guest to bring something to put in the basket. You can pick a theme such as Eliza needing qualities that help her feel better and more in control. Another mom might need more nurturing so you may want to fill her basket with lotion, hairbrushes, and nail polish.

You can fill a basket as a group gift in addition to whatever you choose to do for the Blessingway.

SUGGESTIONS FOR CONTAINING YOURSELF

Filling Mother Shoes: Create a group assemblage of shoes. They can be made from clay or everyone can bring a pair of shoes. Talk about why you chose the pair that you did.
Setting the Stage: Instead of a container, create a stage or plaque that represents the mother's best qualities. Each guest can make something (such as a small clay figurine) to put on the stage. You could make a cooking pot, dancing shoes, or bird wings.
Personal Box: This is a private project. Find or make a box. Put things inside that represent your inner life, the private you. What colors, materials, symbols best represent your inner life? On the outside glue, paint, or design images that represent how you present yourself to the outer world. What are the elements in common to the inside and the outside? What do you hide? How can you bring your inner and outer lives into balance?

Birth Dolls

Each doll reflects the character of its maker; perhaps in the posture and scale of its elements; the fabric selection or stitching style; or the immense display of creative freedom.

- Marthe le Van, *Making Creative Cloth Dolls*

Three pregnant women perched around my big worktable. Baskets of fabric, ribbons and lace, buttons and beads, wires and old pieces of jewelry filled the center of the table. There were needles and thread, scissors, and hot glue guns warming for the job ahead.

Suzanne, Alicia, and Pamela each held a small stuffed doll. The dolls, made of plain cotton, had no fronts or backs, gender, hair or expressions. They were waiting for the women to bring them to life.

Before the women started sifting through the baskets, I had them close their eyes and relax. I asked them what qualities they needed to bring to their pregnancies and births. I asked them to look for colors, textures, and styles. They breathed evenly while they allowed the images to surface. When they opened their eyes, they all knew what they needed to transform their plain figures into birth dolls.

Birth dolls are personal symbols representing qualities or aspects we need or want to be reminded we have. They are allies we can take with us as we journey through the portal of birth. As human-like figures, they are closely aligned with our own self-images. They are mirrors reflecting our strengths. They are also symbols of the children soon to be in our arms and a reminder of our own path from being born to giving birth.

Birth dolls reflect their makers, and so there is no one way to make them. I've made dolls from paper towel tubes and fabric. I've made them from tree branches and handmade paper. I've made them from pre-made forms, and I've sewn my own four-armed mother doll. Each represents some part of me at some time in my life. They represent my own personal journey to motherhood.

The three women at the table searched through the baskets, recognizing what they needed whenever they saw it.

The first thing Suzanne did was to sew a heart-shaped button on her doll's chest. Then she dressed her doll in pink and red and fashioned wings out of lace and wire. She sewed on yellow hair, blue button eyes, and smiling red lips. She named her darling angel doll Mary, after her maternal grandmother. She said Mary was her guardian angel.

Alicia took a very different approach. She outfitted her coffee-colored doll in the brightest prints she could find. She drew big eyes and a big red mouth. Instead of hair, she glued on strips of fabric and decorated her doll, which she named Passion, with beads and baubles. She looked like a high priestess, reflecting Alicia's feelings of being a fertility goddess as she basked in the seductive glow of pregnancy.

Pamela's doll, Serena, wore only a simple green skirt. She had several strands of blue and green beads around her neck and a tiny seashell for a belly button. She represented the ocean to Pamela. She told us she wanted her doll to remind her of the qualities of flexibility, grace, beauty, and simplicity. She liked the idea that even though the ocean was immense, shores held it, and she wanted her birth to have the same qualities.

Each woman's birth doll became an important symbol reminding her of what she needed and wanted as she approached her birth day.

They still occupy a place of honor in these women's homes, even though their babies are now toddlers.

Supplies

1. **Doll bodies**: You can order muslin doll bodies from some doll supply stores, or online at such websites as www.sistersand-daughters.com or www.rosiehippo.com.
2. **Costume**: You need to collect lots of fabric scraps, ribbons, lace, yarn, ribbon, felt, wool roving, handmade paper, raffia, and anything else you like.
3. **Embellishments**: Beads, buttons, pieces of jewelry, seed beads, feathers, leaves, scrap metal, seashells, small stones, pinecones, or anything else that can be glued or sewn on the doll. Ask everyone to contribute a basket full. Before the Blessingway, organize the supplies by type and size.
4. **Decorations**: Fabric paint, markers, rubber stamps, and stamp-pads
5. **Fastening**: Tools for attaching such as a hot glue gun, fabric glue, embroidery and beading needles, regular and beading thread, embroidery thread, scissors, and narrow gauge wire.

Instructions

1. **Time and intention**: Making dolls can take a long time. Give yourselves at least an hour and a half. Consider, too, what you want each person to focus on in her doll making. One idea is to have everyone think about a quality or attribute she possesses —and that her doll can represent. Mom can keep the dolls, a sweet reminder of all her friends' love and support, until a week or so after her baby is born. Then the dolls can be given back to their makers (a great time to return them is when the women come to bring a meal).
2. **Before you begin**: Have everyone sit quietly, eyes closed, breathing evenly and relaxed and ask them to go inside and look for an attribute they would like to bless the mother-to-be with as she becomes a mother. Then, like the women in the story above, they can decorate and dress their dolls accordingly.

3. **Name**: I highly recommend naming your doll. It adds a whole dimension of personalizing and connection. Use your baby-naming book to look up meaning of names.
4. **Parallel activities**: Since this project takes some time to complete, you'll need to stay focused. One activity that blends in well is to go around and have each person tell a story. You can tell about how you met the mother-to-be and how you became friends. If you have mothers as guests, they can tell their birth stories. Everyone else can tell the story of when she was born. By talking about one topic, it will keep the Blessingway focused on the mother-to-be. Try not to let it become too much of a gab session—keep it a group activity. After you are done (or your allotted time is up) go around the room and describe your doll's attributes and her name. Have someone take notes.

Tips

1. **Hair**: You can make hair out of anything: strips of fabric glued or sewed on, yarn sewed down in loops, thin wire shaped into curly-cues, or a row of feathers. Hair does not have to cover her head like yours does. You can just put it around the face creating a suggestion of hair. You're making a doll that reflects your inner life, not making a life-like doll (that's a whole different project).
2. **Faces**: Faces give your doll personality. Button eyes are playful. Painted pouty red lips are sexy. You can paint, draw, or sew on eyes, noses, mouths cheeks, and moles! Some dolls show no facial features, some have wrinkles.
3. **Home**: Where will your doll live? You can design your doll's environment as another aspect of the qualities she (or he) brings to you. Suzanne's angel could be hung from a fishing line or wire above her bed. Alicia's doll, Passion, had her own little table. Alicia covered the table with a piece of African fabric and added little wood animal figures and a candle.
4. **Pockets**: Sew or glue a dream pocket or blessing pocket on your doll. You can write down your dreams for your child and let your doll keep them safe.

Alternatives

Plantation Hanky dolls: In the later 1700s there were few children's toys, so mothers made simple dolls out of men's handkerchiefs which were quite large in those days. The simplicity of this project adds to its beauty. You can use store-bought handkerchiefs or cloth napkins or scraps of fabric such as silk (though the dolls will have a cleaner look if the edges are hemmed). Get the largest you can find—sixteen inches is about as small as you can go.

- Before you tie the fabric into a doll shape, have each guest write or draw a blessing on the inside of the fabric. Don't forget to sign it. Go around the circle and share your blessing with the mother-to-be. You can also sew or glue on lace, fringe or any kind of trim to the bottom edge while you are doing this.
- To make the doll, lay the handkerchief out to form a square. Put a ball of cotton or wool in the center of the hanky. Tie a ribbon or embroidery thread to create a neck. Tie the two top corners to make arms. Tie another piece of ribbon at the shoulder joint (for a more "angelic" look, tie at wrist). Then tie ribbon around the waist to make it look like a body.
- You can leave the dolls sweet and simple like the original "church dolls" (they were given to little girls as a quiet play toy while they attended all-day church). Using an embroidery hoop or twig wreath, tie the dolls on in a descending circle and hang it above the baby's bed to shower her or him with the many blessings the dolls possess.
- You can also dress-up these dolls by painting or drawing on faces or by adding embellishments such as hair and clothes. Have fun!

Magic Wand

Walking through an exhibit on Hindu art, I stopped at an ancient clay sculpture of a goddess. No ordinary goddess, this one had four arms and a necklace of skulls. Kali, Hindu goddess of both creation and destruction, holds a sword in one hand, the head of a demon she has slain in another, and the other two are invitations to her sacred nature.

Her four arms represent the cycle of life—from birth to death. She is the Hindu Divine Mother Goddess. Later, when I learned more about Changing Woman from the Navajo stories, I could see the similarities between them. Like all mothers and those becoming mothers, bringing forth a child means we walk between the forces of life and death. And as mothers we have the ability to nurture and to destroy. No wonder it's so tumultuous to become a mother.

I was intimidated at first, and a bit horrified by her destructive forces. But slowly, as I read the explanations of Kali, I recognized her in me. In my hands, I hold not swords but spoons, representing the nourishing aspects of motherhood. Though I longed for four arms many a day, I learned to do a lot with the two I have. But holding a spoon was not enough, though I did not want to hold a demon's head. I wanted to be more than a pot-stirrer.

I thought long and hard about how to transform my spoon into a symbol representing all the aspects of who I am—mother, yes, but a woman first and a wife, a writer, a dancer, and much more. So I took my spoon and I turned it into a wand. Not as magical as Harry Potter's wand, but transformative enough for me.

The first wand I made came from a large wooden spoon. I decorated it with ribbons and stars. I wrapped scraps of silk around the handle and tied on little bells. I wave it around whenever I need a reminder that I am a whole mother.

If you're looking for some perspective as you enter the mother world, and especially if this is not your first child, making magic wands could be the perfect project for your Blessingway. You can make a bouquet of wands to keep on your birth altar or have everyone take hers home and wave it around her house.

Supplies

1. **Base**: You can buy a bunch of wooden spoons or other wooden kitchen tools as your base, or you can collect pieces of driftwood or thin tree branches. You can ask each person to bring her own, or provide a wide assortment.
2. **Decorations**: Like many of the other examples, you can decide if you want a theme, such as objects from the sea, or you can

gather an assortment of whatever you find yourself attracted to. It may help to ask your guests to contribute as well.

3. **Glue**: Glue-guns and glue sticks (make sure you have cords that will reach your work space).

4. **Scissors**

Variations

1. **Staff**: You can make a staff instead of a wand. Choose a stick at least two inches in diameter and have everyone add something to it. You can hand each person a ribbon or leather cord to string on beads, charms, or other small items.

2. **Magic spells or incantations**: Ask each person to write down a magic spell or incantation symbolizing a quality or skill they wish for you. Karly sent her friend, Bea, a wand wrapped in glitter with play jewels glued all over it. She wrote that the wand was to remind Karly of the brilliance within her and around her.

Stepping Stones

Quietly walking through your garden or backyard, you step on a path of stepping-stones, each image below your feet a lovely reminder of your family, both near and far. The first stone has your own handprint along with your partner's. The fingers gently touch each other, encircled in a colorful frame of polished glass stones. You take a step to the next, three hearts made from pieces of tile, are intertwined in the center, reminding you of the child wiggling inside you that came from your love. The next stone is a spiral of names—your mother and father, your partner's mother and father—the lineage that you both came from and that continues through you as you wait for your new baby. The fourth stone has paw prints and a dog biscuit imprint along with your dog's name. The last stone is scattered with stars; it reminds you of your connection to the universe. Each time you walk among the stones of life, you see your own story cast before you—enduring, vibrant, and distinctive.

Stepping-stones can symbolize the passage you are making from maiden to mother. Make three stepping-stones, the first representing your past, your childhood, who you were as a young girl. You could put in tiny toys or write the names of your favorite books or activities.

The second stone symbolizes the present; it is who you are now, pregnant with your baby, or about to bring home an adopted child. You might put in certain colors or symbols of an animal you relate too. When I was pregnant with my third child, I kept dreaming that I was a sea otter and I gave birth in a swaying bed of kelp. Indeed, my daughter slipped from me after only minutes of labor. My stone would have had pressed sea fronds (or something that looked like seaweed) and a border of shells and a blue glass. I like the sea otter—she is a good mother, attentive and loving. She is playful and powerful. She lives in the ocean among dangerous things but she has found a safe home in the soft hands of the kelp beds.

The third stone is your future—who will you be as mother? This one may be the most fun to do as a group. You can ask each friend to bring a small symbol of your attributes as a mother. Friends can often see what we can't.

If you make the first two before the Blessingway, than after you have made the third stone, you can step from stone to stone on the path to motherhood, pausing at each step and sharing the significance of the objects and words embedded in it with your circle of friends.

Casting stepping-stones is also a great project for a family Blessingway. All ages can contribute stones, tiles, glass, or other outdoor-appropriate materials for making stepping-stones.

Supplies

1. **Concrete**: Craft stores carry small bags of cement and kits just for making stepping-stones. You can also get quick-setting Portland cement from a hardware store.
2. **Mold**: Craft stores carry these in all kinds of shapes—hearts, rounds, squares, half-moons, etc. You can also use deep pie pans (over two-inch deep) or large plastic containers in whatever shape you like. Smaller shapes, such as brick-sized rectangles, can be used for edging or be incorporated into a decorative wall. You can also use cardboard boxes such as a pizza box.
3. **Coating**: Vaseline or other grease to make it possible to take the stone out of the mold when it dries. Make sure you liberally cover the sides, corners and bottom.

4. **Decorations**: Broken pieces of china, polished glass, seashells, marbles, beach glass, mosaic tiles, buttons, small toys, and mementos of any sort. Don't use wood items as they don't stick well and they will deteriorate.
5. **Prints**: You can use cookie cutters, leaves, or other objects to make prints, along with handprints and paw prints.

Directions

1. **Plan your design**: Plan and lay out your design before mixing the cement. Quick-setting cement is just that—quick setting, so you won't have a long time to fool around with changing your design. Children's coloring books have simple designs that may work for you.
2. **Set up your workspace**: Put a board under the mold so that you can move it easily. The person mixing and pouring the cement should wear a construction mask or bandana over their mouth and nose.
3. **Follow the directions for mixing the concrete**: The consistency should be fairly thick, like cookie dough. You want impressions to stay intact. Pat or tap the mold to get all the air bubble out.
4. **Strengthen the stone**: Put down a layer of wire screening or some kind of hard cloth after you've poured about half the cement in.
5. **Have fun making prints**: press in decorations and write names or messages. Allow the cement to dry a few minutes if it's too wet to take your prints.
6. **Drying**: Though the directions usually say to wait twenty-four hours for the mold to dry, it will be stronger and less likely to break when you remove it from the mold if you wait for three days.

Belly Cast

The first Blessingway I ever attended was for my friend Tina. She was one of my first friends to get pregnant and we didn't know what to do for her—she wasn't a traditional baby shower kind of girl. But Tina knew what she wanted. She invited five women friends to make her a belly cast. While I had made face casts and happily decorated them, a belly cast was much more intimate and big.

Tina, a dancer and artist, was happy to show us the way. Though we didn't know about having a circle or offering blessings, we could take care of Tina. We made sure her living room was warm and got her settled comfortably on an old shower curtain covering her couch. One friend rubbed Vaseline all over her belly. She was near her due date and her skin looked like it was ready to burst. She looked incredibly sensual and to my virgin eyes, almost unreal. The avant-garde jazz music Tina was playing awoke my sense of sound. All my senses were awakened and I gobbled up every sensation, aware that I would not be the same again.

Dipping our six-inch-long strips in warm water, we quickly (since these are quick-drying you only have about fifteen minutes before it will start hardening) covered Tina's glistening belly and breasts. As the warm water cooled, she got a little chilled so we draped a towel across her shoulders. Tina decided to put her left hand on her belly and we used small pieces to make sure we could see the detail in her fingers. Tina was sitting so her cast would be as big as she was. Don't lay the pregnant mom on her back—it's neither safe nor will you get a good cast. And remember that she will need to remain still for at least twenty minutes, so make sure she goes to the bathroom first!

Once the cast started to pull of her skin, we carefully loosened the edges and lifted it off her belly. After she went to the bathroom, we looked at it and talked about what she was going to do next.

Most women let the cast dry for a couple of days and then apply gesso, which creates a smoother painting surface. Then, sometimes with their partners, they paint and decorate their cast. Tina liked the simplicity of the cast as it was and decided not to decorate it. Instead, she hung it on the wall in her living room and put a light behind it. It was wild and confident- just like Tina.

Supplies

1. **Plaster impregnated gauze bandages**: Available in medical supply stores or included in belly cast kits. These are fast drying and inexpensive. Buy more than you think you'll need. If you choose thinner strips (two-three inches), you'll need eight-twelve rolls depending on how large the mother is and if you plan to cast just her belly and breasts. If you go further up (or

down) and do her shoulders, upper arms, or thighs, you'll need several more rolls. If you use wider rolls (four-six inches) you'll need around five rolls.

2. **Soft rags** to cover her pubic hair and underarms. You may also want to put the jelly on her pubic hair—it will hurt to get pulled out. The edges of the cast can rub, so be sure to protect her skin.

3. **Un-petroleum jelly** or other water-soluble jelly

4. **Plastic sheet** or old shower curtain

5. **Dishpan** or some kind of plastic pan to dip gauze strips into along with warm water.

6. **Gesso** (acrylic painting primer) and brush

7. **Decorations** such as paint, colored tissue paper, photos, or other kinds of pictures, as well as feathers, shells, beads, fabric, or anything else you'd like that can be glued on. You can apply tissue paper (cut into squares or torn into pieces) before the gauze dries for a dappled effect.

Seeds of Change-gardens

"Plants grow in spite of the gardener. The supreme example of this self-satisfying illusion that gardeners perpetuate is what they go through when growing from seed. Find me the gardener who doesn't hover over a batch of newly germinated seed with a combination of surprise and wonder and a large modicum of smug pride. Gardening is a fine balance between human intervention and the natural course of things."

—Lauren Springer, *The Undaunted Garden*

Robyn's yard was full of flowers. A row of wood roses lined the path to her front door. Fragrant lavender, cheery Shasta daisies, and proud hollyhocks paraded behind. Robyn loved to sit on her bench swing and feast her eyes. When she was pregnant, she spent hours in the swing, smelling her garden and caressing her growing belly. Her baby was due in June when her garden would be at its peak. She loved the connection between her growing garden and her growing baby. She was even considering naming her child after a plant—Lily for a girl and Reed for a boy.

It was easy for Robyn and her friends to plan her Mother Blessing. They decided to make a garden filled with their blessings. Luckily, Robyn had an available patch she had been trying to grow asparagus in—she had already moved the asparagus to a better area in her backyard.

Robyn added compost to the soil in the little garden under the window. The previous homeowners had made a raised bed with mossy covered rock under one of the bedroom windows. They had used it for an office but she was turning it into the baby's room. It was perfect.

Since Robyn knew what kind of plants would grow in the semi-shady bed the best, she made a list for her friends. She and her husband also bought one plant—a climbing rose along with a decorative trellis. They secured the trellis in the ground and dug the hole for the rose before the Mother Blessing.

Robyn's guests arrived with arms full of food and flowers. They crowded around Robyn as she sat in her swing. Her friend, Tillie, opened the circle by reading a poem about a magical garden. Robyn thought about letting everyone plant their plants wherever they wanted, but then she decided to be more organized. She knew that plants grow best when they are in the right place with the right amount of sun and water. It surprised her when she realized that her child would also need structure and that though she loved the chaotic part of the creative process, she could not live in chaos. She and her baby would need the right conditions.

So Robyn asked everyone to help her create a garden that optimized the potential of each plant. They put the bigger plants in the back and considered how the leaves of the blue penstemon flowers would look against the golden leaves of moneywort. When Robyn was satisfied, they planted their blessings and their flowers one at a time. Each friend planted her blessings, written on a little piece of handmade paper, before she put the plant in the hole. Robyn's friend, Tillie, went last. Instead of a plant, she brought California poppy seeds. She told the women that the seeds represented hope for the future. She said poppies return every spring, spreading their seeds to new parts of the garden. They cast their seeds to the wind, trusting they will land in good soil. Tillie told Robyn that she hoped each flower would shine it's blessing of hope and faith as it filled her garden with bright orange blossoms. She also like the idea that the poppies' influence would spread, much like her baby as it grew and learned to walk and talk and grab stuff and make messes.

The last thing the women did before sharing lunch was to water and mulch the garden. They did this in silence, knowing that soon they would be learning to care for Robyn in a new way and knowing she would grow in whatever way was best for her new family.

Supplies

1. **Plants**: Ask the mother-to-be what she wants in her garden. If she's new to gardening, figure out where to put the garden and determine the amount of sun it gets. Garden centers will be able to direct you to appropriate plants. Choose both perennials (plants that return each year) and annuals (flowers that usually last only one season).
2. **Shovels**, gloves, water, and sunscreen!
3. **Season**: This project isn't suitable for a winter Blessingway (unless you live in the South) though you can create a small indoor garden or everyone can give a packet of seeds to plant in the spring.
4. **Containers**: Apartment dwellers can do this project by using a container such as a half-barrel. You'll need to carefully select plants that don't get too big. You could do an annual garden or window garden, especially if it's where the mother-to-be can see it. She can use it as a focal point during her labor and a comfort for times when she is nursing.
5. **Black thumbs**: I would not recommend this project unless the honoree likes to garden. You don't want your friend to feel like she can't even keep a small garden alive when she is about to take on the responsibility for keeping a baby alive.

IV

BLESSINGWAYS FOR ADOPTION OR AFTER BIRTH

Lizzie and Eric's Adoption Blessing

Lizzie and Eric waited a long time for the daughter they recently brought home from Russia. The adoption process left them feeling exposed and vulnerable, but when they finally got to hold their six-month-old daughter in their arms, they knew she was bound to them forever.

After the initial euphoria, Lizzie had waves of conflicting emotions. She told Eric, "One minute I feel profoundly grateful to be a mother and the next minute, I feel like a babysitter waiting for the real parents to pick up the baby."

The reality of baby care was hard for her, too. She had read so much and wanted a baby so long, she thought it would come easily to her. "I thought I would be a natural mother, I'd done plenty of baby-sitting and watched my niece several times for my sister, but Ruby's cries were hard for me to understand. I thought I should know better so I felt badly when I didn't."

The adoption counselor had warned them of these kinds of reactions but the reality was hard to handle.

Their closest friends, Marcia and Joe, had been with them through much of their journey to parenthood. After they talked to Eric and LIzzie about what they needed and wanted, they sent out invitations for a Blessingway.

A Blessing for Ruby
Lizzie and Eric want to introduce their new daughter Ruby to their friends and family who have supported them on their long journey to find each other. Please join this happy new family on May 16th at 12 noon at Lizzie, Eric, and Ruby's house on 3 Oak Lane. They already feel they have been given the best gift of all so they kindly request no gifts.
Please RSVP to Marcia or Joe at 111-2222

Lizzie and Eric told Marcia and Joe that they wanted to do something that symbolized the bond they were developing as a new family of three. Marcia shared how other cultures often bury the placenta beneath a tree. Though they didn't have a placenta, they did have a connection and decided to plant a tree in Ruby's honor. Lizzie felt a tree symbolized the new roots they were growing in their home. They liked the idea of finding a tree native to Russia, so they decided to plant three birch trees. Lizzie read that mythical creatures, sometimes called geniis, loved the Russian birch forests. She also liked the fact that birches grow best in groups.

Joe and Eric spent an afternoon digging deep holes for planting. While they worked, Eric talked to Joe, "You know, Joe, part of me had given up on becoming a father. We tried everything and it just didn't seem to be in the cards for us.

"At some point I stopped hoping," he told Joe. "And now that Ruby's here, part of me doesn't believe that I am really her father. I've only been a dad for a month, and already I feel that I'm not doing my job."

Joe stopped digging to look at his friend. "Eric, my father was one of those 'distant' dads, and I have been afraid to have a child for fear that I would end up being like my father. But you're not like that. I've seen the way you hold Ruby and look at her. I wish my dad had held me that way. You are already a good dad, even if you don't know it yet."

Joe shoveled another load of dirt. Eric wiped the sweat off his face, and with it a few tears.

The next afternoon the guests arrived bearing gifts and congratulations. Many of their friends and family had wanted to do something but didn't know what to do—this Blessingway felt right. After everyone had arrived, Joe asked all of them to come out to the backyard and make a big circle around the tree. Marcia had already passed out leaf shaped paper and markers. Joe hit a drum three times as a way of opening the ceremony. "We are gathered here in honor of Lizzie, Eric and little Ruby. Most of us have waited many years for this chance to bless your new family and we are so glad the day has arrived.

"We know that you two have gone through a long, hard road to get here, and we acknowledge your persistence and commitment to stay together and make your dreams come true. Today we welcome Ruby into not only your life, but to all our lives. We are so glad to have your daughter here with us, in our circle of friends."

Marci put her arm around Lizzie, whose emotion was clear on her face. Eric held Ruby in his arms. Joe continued, "Lizzie and Eric have decided to plant these three beautiful birch trees to symbolize the new life they are starting with Ruby. They asked me to ask you to take a minute and write down a blessing or a wish or a prayer for them."

Someone handed Lizzie a tissue box and several more hands reached for tissues as they all wrote down their blessings for Ruby and her parents.

"Before we hear what you write and you place it among the tree roots, Eric's parents wanted to say something," Joe explained.

Eric's parents held a small Russian nesting doll and told everyone that they were thrilled to be grandparents and wanted to plant the doll to remind Ruby that they knew that as she grew up, she would have much to teach them, and they were eager to hear what she had to say. "We want Ruby to know that she is blessing to all of us," Eric's mom said. Together they gently nestled the doll in the roots.

Each guest read what he or she had written and then tossed the leaf into the hole. "Outdoor play," said one dad. "Lots of hiking and biking."

"A good sense of humor like her dad," said another friend.

"A good heart," said a friend's twelve-year-old daughter.

Eric and Lizzie added their own blessings for Ruby, "My wish for you is to grow up knowing that you are loved and to find strength in our love to be whoever you are meant to be. We love you Ruby and we are so glad you've come."

Then they poured a shovel full of dirt onto the roots. In silence, the shovel went from hand to hand as everyone sealed in his or her blessings.

Back in the house, as Eric and Lizzie's friends ate and talked, they wrote about their Blessingway in a spiral bound book so that no one would ever forget Ruby's blessings.

Honoring the New Parents

Adoption Blessingways can be held before the new parents receive their baby.

Meaningful ceremonies are, by definition, a personal experience. Some parents want to wait until they know they have a healthy baby before celebrating their arrival. Adoption brings a whole new set of customs and decisions. Because adoption can involve both the birth mother and the new parents, or different countries and lots of bureaucracy, ceremonies for the new family are particularly poignant. It's never easy to adopt. People often expect that having children will be an intimate, personal decision, but the path of adoption involves a much more public process. Friends and family may be involved in the adoption decision, and the all the bureaucratic processes of adoption can involve a degree of scrutiny that can feel intrusive and unnerving.

In addition, parents, friends, and family may all have questions about whether or how this new child can truly belong with these parents, this family, and this community. Whatever differences exist between the child's biological family and the adoptive family—class, race, and culture —can become a focus for this concern about belonging. And because adoption can take so long, there can be many intense wishes and hopes for the new parents about what having a new child can bring.

All the wondering, waiting, and wishing takes form in the child. A new family is born and like all new families, all the members have to learn their new roles, new identifies, and new names. A Blessingway ceremony offers the family and its community a wonderful opportunity to honor the difficult journey the parents have taken, and to celebrate their new lives. Adopting ceremonies tend to be about both the child and the parents, and so the activities reflect that as in Lizzie and Eric's tree-planting ceremony for Ruby.

All of the activities I described for pregnant women can be modified to work for an adoption welcoming ceremony. The elements are the same, as are the blessings. Blessingways are ceremonies honoring people for significant rites-of-passage, and becoming a mother or father is one of the most significant.

Some parents want to have a welcoming ceremony, especially if their child came from another country. They want to welcome her or him to a whole new world. Others prefer a smaller more intimate blessing. They may feel that they have "performed" for others (fertility specialists, adoption counselors) long enough.

If your child was internationally or inter-culturally adopted, incorporate the country's songs, poems, rituals, foods, and decorations. This can be a symbol of your intent to honor the culture and traditions of your child's heritage. Don't forget to weave elements from you own culture. It's important to find a balance between honoring your child's culture of origin without making him or her the only member of your family with a culture. International adoptions have become much more common. The number of international adoptions by Americans is now over 20,000 a year, according to the U.S. Department of State. Most of those children come from China, Russia, Ukraine, and Guatemala. It's a small but growing percentage of the approximately 120,000 children who were adopted in 2003 by Americans.

Chad and Denise, parents to two young children, felt that they had room in their lives and in their hearts for more children. As active members of their church they wanted to make a difference in someone's life, and so they made the choice to adopt a child from China. It took months of waiting before they got word that the paperwork had cleared and they could go pick up their daughter. "By the way," their caseworker said, "could you take her younger sister as well?"

Chad and Denise's church community wanted to welcome their families' new members. Between members of the congregation, along with other friends, they expected between seventy-five and a hundred people.

As each guest arrived at the church, they were given a votive candle to light and carry into the sanctuary. The room slowly filled with light and love and friends. Since most of the people were comfortable sitting in the church, they waited silently for everyone to arrive.

Several of their closest friends "officiated" at the ceremony. Their friend Sean began by asking everyone to stand and to sing together. They had printed programs, including lyrics to the songs they planned to sing. The first song was a song of greeting, and at the end they asked everyone to shake hands with at least four other people to greet them. Then they all sang a song from the hymnal.

Sean invited everyone to sit back down, and he began to speak about why they were all there and how honored they were to be witnesses to the commitment this family of four was making to their new daughters and sisters. Several of Chad and Denise's closest friends spoke, including one of their children's friends. Chad and Denise's children handed their new sisters little wooden boxes that they had painted. "These are for your dreams and your memories," they whispered.

Denise's sister talked about how much two more children would change their lives. "You'll need to get a minivan," she joked, "And learn how to speak Chinese."

Ginny read a poem about adoption from *Peach Girl: Poems for a Chinese Daughter* by Joan Siegal and J. Solonche.

Acrostic for Our Daughter, June 1995
By Joel Solonche

Even before you had a name, we began
mothering and fathering the future,
imminent, born twenty months before,
lying bundled, head to foot with another one.
You, our unknown daughter, our Chinese puzzle,

remember always the difficult beginning of us.
Smell the first blossoming flower of being daughter.
First and only daughter, first and only child,
all we had of you we made. We made
a you of a name we loved and many wishes.

Where is Ningbo? You are there.
Come for me in Ningbo, we hear you call.
This way, this way, we hear you call
Calling to us from Ningbo, and
To you we call, Soon we are coming to Ningbo.

Under a tree I write this poem for you,
and many birds are singing around me,
and I imagine you here under the tree also.
Will you be standing here or there by the peonies?
Did you imagine us, mother and father, and

where we would sit with you there? And did
you imagine also, many birds, many birds
singing around us? I think you hear six
small birds singing around you now,
with your name, Emily, their song.

Before they all headed for the potluck reception, they sang a simple lullaby and while they continued to sing, each friend came up to the front where the family of six sat and placed their hands upon their heads to bless them.

Chad and Denise knew that they had a lot of adjusting and learning to do and they knew that they would not be alone, not in body, mind, or spirit.

Portal to Motherhood

Since mothers who adopt don't give birth, society acts as if there's no post-partum period. There is, but it's different. "There's a lot of physical grief present for most moms adopting since most tried to get pregnant before they adopted," explains Lucy, an adoptive mother and therapist. "I know I felt inadequate as a mother since I couldn't get pregnant. It makes me sad that I didn't give birth to my daughter, and I had to work through my grief in order to really bond physically with her." Though not the same kind of physical process as pregnancy and birth, there is a physical as well as emotional and mental aspect to becoming a mother.

Lucy and her partner had a baby blessing ceremony when their daughter was about a month old (they took her home the day after she was born). They asked their friends and family to help them raise their beautiful daughter. Each person shared their blessings and then Lucy put on a CD she'd made and everyone danced, passing baby Molly from loving arms to loving arms and swaying to the rhythms of life. It was a public declaration of the physical reality of being a new parent in the midst of a caring and connected community. Lucy also asked Molly's godparents to stand and acknowledged their presence in Molly's life.

Women who've waited for a long time to have a child often expect to immediately bond with their new child. But, just like any new mom, attachment takes time. It's a process, not an event, and you need to remind yourself daily that you are not a bad mother because you aren't welling up with tears of joy every time you see your child.

Parents in the United States have adopted more than 230,000 children from other countries since 1989.

You probably don't expect your new child to bond instantly to you. After all, they've already had to deal with being given away (sometimes with integrity and sometime not) in their young lives. Give yourself the same grace period of adjustment. You have to adjust to more than just dealing with night feedings or car seat questions. Give yourself time to go through the portal of motherhood.

You may also feel inwardly focused in the first few weeks and months of parenthood as you figure out who you are in your new role, and who you want to be. It may be difficult to be private, especially if, like Loretta, your child is a different race than you. "I get a lot of people asking me questions like, 'Where is he from?' or 'Where did you get him?' Sometimes I don't mind answering, especially if it's someone who is considering interracial adoption as well, but sometimes it feels very invasive."

Mother or family blessings can help. The first step is to acknowledge the journey you have taken. Yearning for a child may have filled your heart for years. Now it's time to learn to love your child as a unique person. It's also time to learn who you are as a parent. What a perfect time to invite close friends to bless your new position in the community. You are now a mother.

Birth Mother Rituals

Most domestic adoptions are open these days—meaning the birth mother (and sometimes father) meet and often choose who is going to raise their child. A mother who gives her child up for adoption can benefit from some kind of ceremony honoring her choices.

The night before Tara was going to give her infant daughter to Veronica and Frank, she got a card from her best friend Chelsea that said, " I know it's hard. You did the right thing. I can only imagine what you're going through. I respect and admire so much who you are to have given her life. I'm here for you."

In the morning Tara changed her baby's diaper one more time, dressed her in a new pink ruffled dress with a sheer cape and little white satin shoes. She had gone to five stores to find the perfect outfit.

Tara rode with her caseworker to the park she had chosen to give her baby to her new parents. She knew she would pass the park often and wanted to be reminded by the majestic trees and soothing grass. They were waiting for her along with a minister, some of their friends, and some of Tara's friends. She held her baby as she slowly walked down the sloping curved sidewalk. It was the first time she walked with her baby in her arms.

Veronica loved the outfit that Tara had chosen, "Where did you get that?" she asked. The shoes were way too big so Tara took them off.

One of Veronica's friends started videotaping, tears streaming down her face. Tara tried not to cry—she wanted to feel good when she saw the tape one day. The minister gave a traditional Christian blessing. He thanked Tara for her courage and generosity and he recognized Veronica and Frank for their open hearts.

Before Tara let go of her daughter, she went to a quiet shady bench to say goodbye alone. She put her hand up, "I'm trying to keep the sun out of your eyes," she told her baby as she looked down at her little red face. She heaved a sigh as she watched her baby flail her arms around curiously. "You're going to have an awesome life," Tara told her, beginning to cry after holding it together for so long. "I've picked out some great parents for you. And I'll see you again some day." That was all she could manage before she broke down. She kissed her on the cheek and smudged the lipstick off before turning around. She hoped no one would notice her shoulders shaking.

Tara brought her baby, whose middle name she chose and Veronica and Frank decided to keep, back to the group. She couldn't look anyone in the eye as she put her daughter in Veronica's arms. Her tears turned into sobs and her friends hugged her.

Tara couldn't hear Veronica and Frank's gratitude and promises. Her friends walked her back to the car. She had planned to leave first so she wouldn't have to watch her baby being taken away.

She stayed with her friend Chelsea that night and told her birth story over and over. Chelsea brushed her hair, brought her tea, and listened. Eventually, she could talk about the placement ceremony.

Teresa brought a pile of freshly washed newborn T-shirts and a basket of embroidery thread and needles. While the guests shared their blessings, they embroidered simple designs on the shirts.

Tara says, "It helped me say goodbye although you never really say goodbye. Four years later, I still get letters, emails, pictures, videos, cards, and gifts from my daughter and I send the same."

Tara doesn't know what kind of ceremony Veronica and Frank did to welcome their baby, whom they named McKenzie. Tara knows she is included in the family tree. Since this was an open adoption, McKenzie knows she has two mommies who love her—one who gave birth to her and one who takes care of her now.

There are many ways of creating a family. Robin, whose adult daughter has developmental disabilities, is adopting her seven-year-old grandson. Lisa and Wendy used a sperm donor. Jackie and Dana adopted their daughter from Mexico, though Jackie had to adopt as a single mother since Mexico does not allow gay couples to adopt.

Ceremonies

TREE PLANTING

Lizzie and Eric's tree-planting ceremony crossed cultures and generations. It included all the people who'd been waiting for Ruby and had supported Lizzie and Eric throughout the long process.

Trees have their own symbolism—they live a long time and become focal points in yards and gardens. But you can plant bushes and flowers as well. Rose bushes are a popular choice to plant in someone's name. In the projects section of this book, I describe how to plant a garden for a new family. You can ask everyone to choose plants from a list you provide (so that they are compatible and can grow in the place you plant them) and then each person can plant a blessing with their individual plant.

Another approach is to plant more than blessings with your tree or bush. You could plant little symbols of the qualities or attributes you wish for your new family such as a feather to symbolize not taking things too seriously. Or a cup of ocean water reminding you of your commitment to go to the beach at least once a year. You could put a bead from another country reminding you of your love of travel. You could plant an oak seed representing your hope for patience.

Supplies

1. **Tree, bush, or perennial plant**: Make sure it's suitable to your climate and to the conditions it will get depending on where you plant it (sun, soil Ph, water, foot traffic).
2. **Digging supplies**: Shovel, water, gloves, sunscreen, root starter.
3. **Blessings**: Written on paper or symbols.

FLAGS OR BANNERS

Before I had children, my husband and I traveled around the world. Traveling in places where everything is different and unfamiliar opens you to new ways of seeing, feeling, and believing. It's a lot like bringing home a baby. Your senses awaken, time slows down, each day brings adventure (though much of it mundane) as you learn to understand and navigate your new world.

Our travel philosophy is much like our parenting philosophy—try it and see what happens. Sometimes it requires great patience, like when we spent most of a day trying to cross Bangkok. It would have been faster to fly to another country than it was to cross downtown.

Chance meetings change us forever. When we trekked for a month in Nepal our method of trekking was off-kilter with all the other trekkers. The locals laughed at us as we arrived for lunch hours after everyone else that had already come and gone. But what happened is we got to visit with the Nepali people instead of other trekkers. We stayed in the little villages in-between the main trekking ones. We found our own way.

High above tree line, in a Buddhist enclave at the feet of the lofty Annupurnas, we stopped to spend the night. Our hosts, Tashi and his wife Foto, welcomed us so deeply we stayed for three days. And in that time, we learned about their community. Because we stayed, we participated in some of their activities, a rare privilege. We joined them at the Buddhist temple to bless the beasts about to be slaughtered for the Hindu festival of lights. Tashi and Foto also invited us to make Buddhist prayer flags with them.

Using a block print handed down through three generation of Tashi's family, we pressed white muslin onto the inked board. It took two people to make each flag—we sat across from one another and worked together. The flags became sacred only when the monks blessed them. I have two flags hanging in my living room—they still wave the blessings of that magical time.

Prayer flags spread their blessings every time the wind filters through them. They herald gratitude and joy. Flags identify a home as one blessed by community, family, and love.

You can make a row of small flags and hang them across your front door or in your child's room. You can make a banner covered in handprints and wishes and drape it over a wall. You can attach your flags to sticks or stakes and plant them along your walkway. However you make them, blessings flags will blow blessings through you and your home.

Supplies

1. **Fabric squares or rectangles**: You can use white cotton or a rainbow of colors (keep to lighter colors so you can see your painting). You can buy cloth napkins already hemmed (wash first and try to get 100% cotton). You can dye your own fabric to match your décor.
2. **Paint supplies**: You can use fabric or acrylic paints, brushes, fabric pens, stamps, and stencils. Here's where your creativity comes in. You could design a family logo (see below for instructions) and print it on each flag leaving room for friends and family to write their blessings with Sharpie pens or fabric markers. Just let everyone do whatever he or she wants. Ask everyone to draw or stencil their favorite animal and then write the quality or attribute about that animal that most appeals to them. For instance, the giraffe is known as the land animal with

the largest heart. The dolphin is a playful, devoted family member. The spider weaves beauty into her home. If your child has come to you from China, you could copy Chinese characters onto the flags.

3. **Workspace**: As with all paint projects, make sure you have protected your furniture and floors and your guest's clothes. You can use a painter's drop cloth or an old shower curtain or layers of newspaper. Cut pieces of cardboard to put under each flag as it is painted, you can tape the edges down to make it easier to paint and write.

4. **Hanging the flags**: An easy way to hang flags is to fold over the top to create a small sleeve. Sew the sleeve closed or use fabric glue. After it dries, run a study cord or ribbon through each one. Make sure they are all facing the right way. If they slip and bunch up, use a straight pin or a spot of fabric glue to hold them in place. If you want the flags on individual stakes, make a sleeve on one side.

5. **Outdoor use**: Flags hung outside will eventually disintegrate. The Buddhists believe that decay is part of life and it reminds them not to get too attached to things and ideas. If you don't want your flags to decay, then hang them inside, ideally near a window so they can flutter in the breeze.

FAMILY LOGO

We are bombarded with logos every day. Kids can tell you where the fast food places are well before they can read. Our brains are wired to recognize and interpret symbols. Yet we rarely make the symbols, we usually just respond to them. But we can tap into the power of symbols by making our own family symbol or logo.

Family symbols are found in cultures old and new all over the world. In Western Canada and the northwest United States, the coastal Native Americans have used family totems for many generations. In the Haida Indian creation myth, the first two clans were the Eagle and the Raven. The people carved images of these guardian spirits and honored them.

In Japan, there are thousands of family crests. The symbols they use come from plants, animals, nature, architecture, abstract designs, and characters (letters). It keeps families connected to their ancestors and makes genealogy easier to do and understand.

Other cultures such as the Scottish and English have coats of arms that symbolize their family name. Colors, objects, and symbols tell stories through the crest.

Though your child may come to you with a different lineage and culture, he or she has joined your family, giving you an opportunity to create a new logo, crest, or totem.

Designing your family logo may take some time. It could be done as a group or it could be just the parents and child or children. I would recommend that the designing of it be a private process but that it is unveiled at the Blessingway.

Bob and Meredith are very visual people. They love visiting art galleries and decorated their home in bold colors. When they adopted their daughter as an infant, they decided to name her Rose. They planted roses in their yard in her honor. When Meredith buys flowers for the house, she usually chooses roses. Bob gave Meredith a plaque for her birthday–it too had roses.

Roses became their family logo. After a while, they started to use it that way. Bob put a little rose by their names on their holiday newsletter. They hung a banner with a rose on it, outside their house.

When Rose was in first grade, one of her school assignments was to find out why her parents had named her Rose. They told her it was because when they first talked about starting a family, they'd been at a picnic at the botanical garden and walked through the rose garden. The perfume of roses permeated their skin, and in a way, they could feel the presence of their child. It was three years before Rose came, but every time they saw or smelled roses, they felt sure they would have a family. They told her they liked that roses made people think about love and that they knew they already loved her.

There are many ways to create a family logo. Begin by noticing what images or objects you are drawn to. Do you always see dolphins when you go to the beach? Do you seem to find coins wherever you go? Have you filled your home with a certain color or motif? Do you collect stamps or figurines or books by a certain author?

Use what you already know about yourself to create your family symbol. If you like stamps, use that model to design your logo. Think about why you collect the figurines you do. My mother loves cows; they remind her of her father and of growing up on a farm. If you love an author such as Eric Carle—use his technique of making collages out of painted paper for your family symbol. Make a totem.

What you make your symbol out of is so personal I am reluctant to provide a supply list. Your symbol could be an object or something you draw or design on a computer. It could be a collage of paper and fabric or a basket of feathers and seashells.

NAME GAME

Naming a child is easy for some parents and agonizingly difficult for others. My brother-in-law and his wife took over a week to name their sons and even then, they couldn't agree on nicknames. One of the boys changed his own name when he was seven.

Some people know the name of their child their whole lives. Elizabeth had no doubt she would name her daughter Sidney. But she never used the name—it didn't fit any of her three sons.

Family names are usually considered in the naming game, both first and last. Cathy and Wheaton gave their daughter her last name and their two sons his last name. Teresa and Karen, a lesbian couple, hyphenate their last name for themselves and their daughter.

A name carries a lot of weight. We judge people by their names before we even meet them. We associate names like Candi, Tiffany, and Crystal, as less serious then names like Sarah, Elizabeth, or Julie.

African Americans in the US have a strong tradition of using creative and Afro-centric names. Names reinforce and affirm cultural values. Immigrant families may choose names that reflect the new culture, the culture of origin, or a combination. Each of these choices can reflect the relationship with culture, and hopes for your child's life.

What about your own name? How you feel about your name influences how you pick your child's name. If you've always disliked your name—thought it was too formal or too silly or too weird—you're likely to swing the other way when naming your child.

Try this activity to see how you feel about your name. We can look for a variety of qualities in our names—color, shape, texture, size; all reveal what we think about our names. By turning your name into art, you can see the beauty in every letter. After you and your guests do your own names, make something beautiful together for your child's name.

Supplies

1. **Base Material**: You can use decorative or handmade paper. It's best to have some stiffness, but not as stiff as cardboard unless you do not plan to cut it. If you do want to cut the paper into shapes, do so before designing. You can have everyone start with the same shape and then watch as each one becomes unique when decorated. Guests can make their own names and take them home and do one of the child's first and/or last name so the parents can make a mobile from them or glue them in a scrapbook.
2. **Art materials**: You'll need fabric or acrylic paint, brushes, and markers if it's on fabric. Use pastels, markers, paint, crayons, or glue objects on the paper (you may need to use poster board if you plan to glue).
3. **Display**: Punch three holes on one side and tie it with a colorful ribbon. Put them in a scrapbook along with photos of the Blessingway and written blessings. Hang them like flags across your child's room.

Instructions

1. **Consider**: Think about why you were given (or took) your name. Do you like your name? Do you go by a nickname or version of your name? (If you name is Elizabeth, do you go by Liz or Beth or Bess?) What name does your family of origin call you? Is it different than the name your partner uses, or your friends?
2. **Design**: Once you've thought about your name and everyone else you've invited has done the same, create a design using your name. Use whatever materials you like—pastels, paint, markers, torn paper, objects.

3. **Time**: Allow ten-fifteen minutes to do this first part. You want enough time to work with your child's name. If she or he had a given name, you can make a design with that name. Give everyone more time to do this design. You can do just first names or both first and last. Ask everyone to write down what they felt about the name while they were creating the design.
4. **Display**: You can make a book out of the pages or glue them into a scrapbook. If you do the designs on fabric, you can make a blessing flag from them.

PICTURE TREE

Sobunfu' Some is a spiritual teacher and the author of *Welcoming Spirit Home: Ancient African Teachings to Celebrate Children and Community*. She grew up in a tiny village in Burkina Faso where every woman was her mother, every man her father, and every child her brother or sister. Sobunfu' says that one of the best ways to create a loving home is to welcome each member when they arrive. She says to welcome them with a hug or kiss and ask how they are doing. She says to do this every time they come home; they must be greeted this way. When they leave, their departure should also be acknowledged. No slipping out the door. It's a beautiful custom.

Since we no longer live in villages where everybody knows our name, we have to find other ways to bring home the faces of our extended families.

One way is to create a family picture tree. Ask every member of your family to send you a picture of them or go through your own pictures. Ask that they also send a blessing written on a beautiful piece of paper. Glue the two together back-to-back, punch a hole in the top, thread it with a piece of ribbon or raffia and hang the "leaves" on a bouquet of branches arranged in a vase. Place your picture tree where everyone can be seen and welcome them home.

Family trees don't have to be hung; they can also be mounted and framed. Put your child's picture at the top, then the parents and sibling(s), then grandparents, aunts, uncles, cousins and great-grandparents. To make your own, you'll need to figure out how many people you want to include. It can get very large.

This brings up another issue about how to include the people who are absent or uninvolved. Do you include the birth mother and father? The egg or sperm donor? Perhaps a symbolic representation of the people is a way to acknowledge the fact that without them your child would not be here. Maybe you noticed a robin on your lawn the day you found out you were going to be a parent—you could use that image to represent the gift of life she (or he) gave your family.

Supplies

Family Tree

1. **Photos**: If you ask people to send whatever they want you will get a wide range of sizes, focus and contrast. I rather like that; to me it reflects how that person sees himself or herself. It reveals more than a face. You can ask for all photos to be no bigger than 4x4 inches. Don't go to a standard 4x6 inches photo as there is likely to be a lot of background that you'll have to crop to make the face stand out. Request that the face be at least one inch so that you'll be able to see them easily.
2. **Blessings**: Once you decide on the size of your leaves, send a piece of special paper to each person in your family. You can include it in an adoption announcement. Have them write a blessing, a wish, a quality, or a poem to your child.
3. **Borders and backing**: The leaves will look better with a border. The easiest thing is to glue them on the back of a piece of thick handmade paper about half an inch bigger than the photo. You could also use felt, craft foam, or paper frames. You can also trim the photo with craft scissors – it will give it a playful look.

V

PREPARING BODY, MIND, AND SOUL

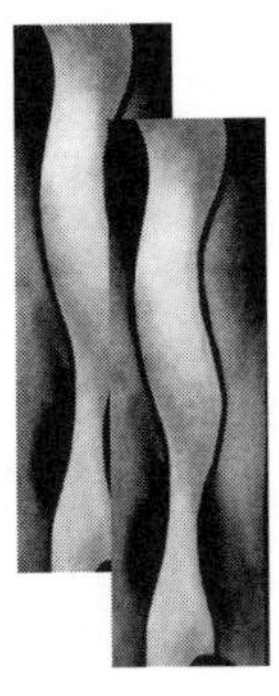

In the seconds that it takes for the two purple lines to appear on a home pregnancy test, a women's life is forever changed whether or not she's ready. Immediately, she must begin to make choices—coffee or not, tell anyone or not, keep it or not. Most pregnant women begin by collecting information. Birthing books, doctor's advice, childbirth classes, our mothers—all help a women feel that if she collects enough facts, if she does her Kegals and squats, if she picks the right caregiver and if she learns to breathe right, that birth will be something she can manage.

My own first pregnancy parallels this experience of middle-class women who excel at taking care of things. I read every book I could find, hired a doula, practiced my Kegals, and thought constantly about the birth. What I didn't really consider was the fact that birth would be only a day (I hoped) and my transformation into motherhood would be forever. I was prepared for the birth but not ready for the baby.

Birth is a portal, and the way through is indeed a potent rite-of-passage, not only for mom, but for dad (or partner), baby, and the new family that is formed. Consciously moving through this doorway is important. So is understanding that a woman's ability to shape and control the experience is mostly an illusion. Though much of pregnancy and birth is not controllable, you can manage much of it, such as what you wear or whom you have with you.

Pregnancy is, for most women, the first time that they cannot force themselves to control their body. Morning sickness, heartburn, or swollen ankles cannot be willed away. The pregnant body, stretched from within, is playing the role of host to this new person. Our bodies, which many have starved and certainly have fretted over, are now running the show.

For me and for women everywhere, having a baby was the greatest teacher of learning to trust my body. My mantra for my first birth was "surrender." I did not want to collapse, but to sink into the physical sensations. What I learned in surrendering to birth, I carry within me as I learn to surrender to the journey of mothering.

When the contractions finally started, they were long and hard. I went from eating breakfast to active labor in about an hour. I stood moaning in the shower telling my unborn son we could do this and asking him what he needed. When my doula arrived and realized I was in transition, we rushed to the hospital. The nurses wanted to take control of my birth, wanted me on the bed, wanted a monitor on me, told me when and how to push.

Pushing burned like a fire, so I again told myself to "surrender." It still hurt, but I was able to allow my baby's head to emerge. He was perfect and so very welcome.

A newborn's awakening is all physical—the first breaths, the first gaze into her mother's eyes, the first taste of sweet milk. Our bodies are the bridge between the sacred and the profane. We need to eat and we often need to pray. So we begin with our bodies.

My experience with moving my body—whether through dance, yoga, skiing, or running—is that it somehow frees my mind. It's as if my cells hold me back until I give them a chance to breathe. Then the wisdom of my body reveals what my mental editor has kept from me. We awaken, like the newborn, by moving with awareness, noting all the thoughts and sensations that run through our bodies.

Reacquainted with our bodies, we then look for words to describing the experience. In my pregnancy classes, I go from the dance to the paper. Through writing prompts, we allow the words to make sense of our thoughts and to give our feelings names. We might use metaphors such as imagining ourselves to be an animal or a type of weather or a place in nature. Sometimes, we make poems. Sometimes our words turn into essays or songs, and often they become part of the legacy we build for our unborn son or daughter.

After words, there is one more part of ourselves that yearns to be heard—it is our soul. I believe the soul is rightly expressed through creative arts. The individual ability is not important, for though soul longs for form, it is the process of creation itself that is the true quest. The mediums can be anything—paint, sculpture, construction, or pastels. Different mediums do elicit different types of responses. Dream images usually need to be drawn or painted. Clay is superb for giving structure to the unformed questions. It mimics our own pliable physicality. I like the qualities of flexibility, openness and possibility inherent in clay. I describe clay as "holding our truth in our hands" as we shape it into recognizable forms.

Through these three aspects—body/movement, mind/words, and soul/art—exists the potential for greater self-awareness. And when we can see our own patterns and habits, we give ourselves back the option to choose. Choice gives us power. And self-awareness shapes our intentions for our births and our parenting.

To some people dancing, singing, writing poetry, and painting are not as important as getting practical information regarding birth. As a culture that rarely witnesses birth, we do need to get the facts, but the facts do not prepare women emotionally, spiritually, or psychologically for the incredible experience of pregnancy, birth, and motherhood. In my personal experience of birthing three children, and in my work with women becoming mothers, I know that playing with clay may hold the key for one woman to delve into her fears. I've witnessed other women who are transformed in the dance, becoming fertility goddesses right in front of me. I've listened to a poem revealing a women's desire not to have her mother at her birth.

Even greater than the experience of labor and birth is the lifetime role of mother. We can better navigate that tricky terrain through the sacred threshold of pregnancy and birth. I was better prepared to be a mother myself through the dancing, singing, drawing, and writing I did during my pregnancy. There is an art to birthing, and it is in the integration of body, mind, and soul.

Body

We support our bodies by nourishing them with good food, abundant water, gentle touch, conscious movements, beautiful clothes body decorations, and awakening our senses. Earlier I talked about getting massages, immersing yourself in water, dancing, skin care, and aromatherapy. Here, I want to give you some more resources and activities to preparer your body for birth and beyond.

MINDFUL MEDITATION

"Meditation is not about being cross-legged and quiet," said Teresa Robertson, an intuitive counselor. "It's about being in the moment."

Robertson and Mary Bell, director of the Physic Horizons center, taught mediation classes for kids.

"As a teacher," said Bell, "you give kids total permission to be who they are. You are not dictating what they learn. They are learning it themselves and you are watching."

"The more playful you can be," said Bell, "the more quickly you can clear out your space. The only time children lose their space is when someone else is in their head. We teach concentration skills."

The same principles apply to adults. Meditation is about being in the moment, it does not necessarily require stillness and silence.

In their parent-child meditation class I once attended, they taught everyone how to ground their energy. "In your mind's eye," instructed Bell, "imagine a cord or a tail going down from your bottom into the earth. Make it strong."

After getting ourselves grounded, she passed out paper and crayons and asked everyone to draw a picture of our grounding cord. Kids and parents went around the room and shared them with the rest of the group. Parent's and children's pictures were very much alike.

"Now get up and stay with the grounding energy and let's be frogs." I joined them hopping and croaking across the room, our self-consciousness soon giving way to giggles as we strutted like chickens, flew like airplanes, and growled like lions. "This is mediating?" I thought before I realized having fun is usually an act of being in the moment. "Maybe she's onto something."

The classes also help parents learn to give to themselves so they don't burn out. Parenting is not an easy job. "One of the best ways families can stay in communication together," says Bell, "is through meditation. It's fun to be in the moment."

Bell and Robertson gave their students permission to find a way of being present that worked for them. Pregnant women may want to just lie down and listen to ocean music and think about their baby like I did, or they may get up and go out the door and try a breath-walk.

Breath-walk

Pregnant women all over the world walk throughout their pregnancies. Most of the time it's to get from here to there, but occasionally, a woman slows her pace and slows her mind and walks with her breath, which she shares with her baby.

A breath-walk is a walking mediation, much like monks practice. It can be done anywhere but I suggest choosing a quiet place to minimize distraction. Do not carry anything in your hands —they need to swing freely. Wear a backpack on both shoulders if you need to carry water or a sweater. This walk will not make you sweat so dress appropriately.

To begin, stand with your feet about shoulder-width apart. Let your weight spread evenly across the heel and ball of your foot. Relax your jaw and shoulders. Close your eyes and take several deep breaths, in a four-part rhythm:

1. Inhale slowly for a count of four
2. Hold your breath for a count of four
3. Slowly release your breath for a count of four
4. Pause again for a count of four
5. Repeat four times.

On the fifth inhale, step forward, pause, step forward with the other foot on the exhale and pause again. Do that four times.

If you like the slow pace, keep walking this way (though do open your eyes). If you feel impatient, increase the speed by breathing normally and walking in rhythm to your breath. Try both of these paces:

1. Take one step with each foot for each inhale and one step on each foot for each exhale.
2. Take four steps (two each foot) for each inhale.

Play with changing the length of your step. Let your arms hang and swing in reaction to your body movements. Moving mediations require a different way of being in your body. By practicing how to keep your upper body and jaw relaxed while you focus your awareness on your breath and walk in rhythm, you are practicing for labor and taking care of an infant.

Most women can talk and move comfortably through their early contractions. Do a breath-walk with your partner around the block. You could also use your breath to move to music (your own inner choir or a piece you've practiced dancing to already).

By learning how to stay present to your breath while doing something else, you are learning to mindfully multi-task, a skill that will serve you well as you learn to care for a newborns' needs.

Enjoy the walk.

AWAKENING THE SENSES

Pregnancy is an intensely physical time in a woman's life. While much of your time is spent in minimizing symptoms, you can also honor your body by tuning into your senses. Breath-walks are a delightful way to practice meditation in motion. But what about your other senses—smell, touch, sight, taste?

The first trimester is usually not the best time to try some of these, as your body has not yet adjusted to your pregnancy. Try them after morning sickness has faded and you are feeling good again. These ideas can be incorporated into your Blessingway ceremony as well.

1) **Succulent spreads**: Open a package of your favorite crackers or bread. Ask your friends to bring one kind of food to put on the crackers:

   a. Mustard

   b. Cheese

   c. Vegetable spreads (hummus, artichoke dip, etc)

   d. Ginger (pickled, dried and fresh)

2) **Sweet bouquet**:

   a. Make a potpourri of favorite flower scents —ask everyone to bring an herb, oil, or flower of his or her favorite scent. Put them all in a bowl of hot water to steam as you have the Blessingway.

   b. Ask everyone to bring a flower and create an original bouquet, or weave them into a crown.

3) **Soothing sounds**:

   a. Ask everyone to bring a CD with a favorite song and make a tape.

   b. Make a theme tape such as:

      ❖ Favorite lullaby

      ❖ Favorite classical, jazz, or rock song

      ❖ Favorite mother-child song

      ❖ Favorite nature piece

4) **Calm touch**: Traditional Blessingways always include physically nurturing the mother-to-be. Incorporate as many of these suggestions as you can:

Brush her hair
Wash her feet
Paint her toenails
Massage her neck
Give a facial
Soak her hands

5) **Celebrate the seasons**: Connect to the greater cycle of life through the seasons with these easy ideas:

a. Offer the fruits of the season such as strawberries in spring, peaches in summer, pears in fall, and tangerines in winter. Feed them to the mom and each other.
b. Make a seasonal bouquet.
c. Ask everyone to bring a symbol from nature representing the season and ask him or her to explain his or her choice. Create a birth altar.

BELLY ART: BELLY PAINTS, TATTOOS AND HENNA MENDI

Paints

In 2003, the "News of the Weird" reported on the first "belly painting Contest," sponsored by *BabyTalk* magazine. Hundreds of women sent photos in of their big colorful bellies.

Women had painted on sunbursts, the moons and stars, a ticking time bomb, cinnamon buns, and even Michelangelo's famous *Creation* painting (two hands reaching for each other).

The winner was Kelle Steeger, a mother-of-two from San Antonio, Texas. Her belly sported a giant porthole with a baby peering out while wearing a diving mask and snorkel. The artist, her friend Michelle Esparza, regularly paints bellies now: "Some moms get belly molds; others do portraits —this is just another way to enjoy your pregnancy," she said.

Temporary by nature, belly paintings are a delightful form of expression. Paintings can be anything—abstract swirls of color, wild faces and designs, complex compositions. Some women prefer to paint from the baby's perspective, like Kelle did. Others want to go with a recurring theme as such as sea images or wildflowers.

Supplies

1. **Paint**: Use water-soluble face painting crayons or make your own (see below).
2. **Friend or partner**: You can paint your own belly, but if you're close to birth-day, you probably won't be able to reach the underside of your belly. Besides, it's a blast to watch someone else do it. (Body painting has an erotic element to it if you decide to go there.)
3. **Eyeliner pencil**: Use black for outlines. Use other colored eyeliner pencils to add details.
4. **Camera**: The paint won't last but the picture will. Take several shots, both close up and full-body for your mother book.

Recipe for belly paint.

Mix all the following ingredients in a small bowl, Tupperware container, or even in a clean muffin pan.

Make as many different colors as you want!

- ❖ 1 teaspoon corn starch
- ❖ 1/2 teaspoon water
- ❖ 1/2 teaspoon cold cream
- ❖ Food coloring

Tattoos

"Decorating our bodies before labor reminds me of Celtic warriors getting tattooed with blue woad before going into battle," said Karen, a mother of two and a doula. "Self-decoration is a form of personal expression of a mother's hopes and dreams for herself, her baby, and their labor journey. The images chosen can be used to announce to the world, 'Hey! I'm a woman in full blossom, ready to go into labor and prepared for anything.' Or they can be a form of communication from the mother to her baby, like 'I'm decorating my belly with beautiful images that reflect how beautiful I feel with you growing inside me.'"

Karen, concerned that her taut belly skin would not hold a traditional henna tattoo, decorated her belly with fairies, wizards and beautiful flowers. "I loved looking at them the last few days," she said. "During the birth they were a nice counter point to all the frenzied activity (my labor lasted only two and a half hours)—something to catch the eye and stop the observer for a second, checking out all the different pictures on my belly."

One of her clients applied temporary tattoos of red hearts in concentric circles around her belly. "It looked gorgeous and fun and so full of love for her belly and her baby. Unfortunately, she ended up with a C-section and all the hearts had to be washed off before they could do the surgery. The nurses thought it was a nice surprise to see all those hearts."

Henna Mehndi

The women of India have been painting their bodies (mostly hands, feet and face since the rest is supposed to be covered up) for over 5,000 years. Traditionally worn in a ritualized manner for ceremonies and important occasions such as weddings, the art takes a different form in Western countries. While many people like the ancient patterns of swirls and scrolls, they put them in untraditional places like around a pregnant belly.

Jessica McQueen, a henna artist from California says, "Applying henna to the belly toward the end of a pregnancy in certain cultures is believed to protect or bless the mother and child during the difficulties of labor. It's believed to guard against the evil eye and protect from evil or malicious spirits that may be near during delivery."

"If a woman wants to get a henna even in the last months of pregnancy, I would suggest that she go for it if it brings her delight and makes her feel beautiful," encourages Canadian henna artist Luma R. Brieuc.

Henna is made from an herbal compound with no known side effects or reactions. True henna is brown though it will change and fade for the one to four weeks it's on. Some kits offer black henna but it's dangerous to use as its color comes from a toxic chemical dye. Henna is applied using a stencil and a paste made of the plant (most people also add scents). The application process can take anywhere from a few minutes to hours, but it's the setting process that is most time-consuming. Some henna artists recommend leaving the past on for up to eight hours. The longer it's on, the darker the design. While the paste will dry and start peeling, you may need to use some vegetable oil to get it all off. Keep the design out of the water for at least twenty-four hours afterwards, as well.

"During pregnancy, henna stains are not as dark as they could be,"says Brieuc. "It has more to do with the hormonal changes that occur during pregnancy than the 'thickness' of the skin. The hormonal changes affect the ph level of the skin, which in turn affects the darkness of the henna stain. Each woman responds differently, and usually the henna is darker earlier in pregnancy."

McQueen suggests pregnant women use a simple henna recipe to limit irritation. "Use henna powder, lemon or lime juice, sugar, and lavender essential oils," she said. "There is no reason why a medium-dark stain cannot be achieved on a pregnant belly if a good fresh powder with lavender oils is used. Patterns on bellies will always be lighter than on hands and feet, whether pregnant or not. Leaving the paste on for eight hours really helps, four hours would be my minimum."

Henna mehndi can be applied to any part of your skin. Invite a henna artist to your Blessingway and have her put the same "bracelet" or "anklet" on everyone as a symbol of your unity of support for the new mom. When she looks at her own hand during labor, she will be connected to her circle of friends.

"Blessingways and henna parties can be combined into a day of pampering and relaxation for the expectant mom and her friends as well," McQueen suggests. "It is a fun reason to gather the women in your life together for support, encouragement, and a little excitement while celebrating the end of your pregnancy. Plus, everyone has a little reminder of the day together as the designs last seven to ten days."

Brieuc reminds us that henna is a sacred art," When I meet someone to do a henna, I always remember that I am serving through the creative gift that has been given to me, and that I am privileged to enter, for a short lapse of time, an intimate part of the life of the person I am about to henna. I greet any henna experience with sacredness."

McQueen agrees, "Having henna applied, having someone touching your swollen belly, can be very calming. The henna paste is cooling and can help relieve heat exhaustion and sooth hot skin as well as being a natural sun block. Henna brings something restful and joyous to the strenuous last trimester and helps women embrace the transformation and swollen belly.

"Henna during pregnancy celebrates the unique shape of a full belly with expansive patterns that complement the figure.

"The application process of mehndi or henna body art on a pregnant belly is a time where the mom needs to be still and relaxed. She has to find time in her schedule to sit down for a few hours and focus on her belly, on her pregnancy, and her new life. This is a wonderful opportunity to visit with a few close girlfriends before the birth."

Henna Mehndi looks like tattooing, but the experience is painless and pleasant and the effects simply stunning.

FILLING YOUR BELLY

The day we brought our newborn son home from the hospital, our friends Ned and Margaret brought us dinner. I can remember it precisely—a mushroom lasagna, green salad, a loaf of fresh-baked French bread, and a pint of Ben & Jerry's "Cherry Garcia." I was stunned by their incredible generosity. It was one of the most delicious and satisfying meals I have ever had.

Making meals for new parents, for busy two income families, or for those with or caring for an illness, is one of the greatest gifts one can give.

Postpartum mothers need lots of rest, nurturing, and nourishment. Many women focus on the birth, thinking it's all over when the baby is born. But really it has just begun. New mothers need special care in the first few postpartum weeks. They need time to deal with their complex emotions, their changing body, and the awesome task of infant care.

There is little social recognition of what it takes to be a new mother. Some estimate that half of all new mothers suffer from some level of postpartum depression. I think a lot of that stems from our expectations, both society's and our own, to do it all. What we need to do is not easy, especially for a women accustomed to taking care of others. We need to ask for help.

Preparing and delivering meals is a tremendous help. It not only frees up both parents from shopping, cooking, and cleaning, but it provides loving nourishment. No outfit, no matter how adorable, will matter as much as providing meals.

One way to make sure the new family will be fed is to plan it during the Blessingway. Ask friends and family to sign up for a dinner. Not everyone will want or be able to do this, so figure out a graceful way for people not to sign up. Bringing a basket of muffins or a coupon for a delivered pizza is just as supportive and is welcome months after a child is born.

Order the list by Day One, Day Two, and so on, not by day of the week. You won't know when the birth-day is yet. Friends can cook more than once. When the baby is born call the friend in charge of the list. She will then call everyone and tell them that Day Three is now Tuesday. It will take some rearranging, so the person organizing it needs to be flexible but persistent. Discuss dietary needs and wants at the Blessingway. When it's your turn to deliver dinner, keep your visit short and offer any other help if you're so inclined.

Some families leave a cooler by the front door and ask friends not to ring or knock and just leave dinner. Add a note of congratulations or any cooking directions they might need for the dinner. Plan to have a new meal brought every day for the first week then check back in with the parents. They might be swimming in leftovers, and you may be able to have friends bring a meal every other day for the next two weeks. The new mom may also find that certain foods affect her or the baby, so the organizer needs to know this so she can pass the word. Many new moms avoid cabbage, onions, tomatoes, broccoli, and other gas-producing foods.

Nola noticed her baby spit up more whenever she ate raw spinach or lettuce, so she stopped eating them. She ate cooked spinach and slowly introduced raw greens back into her diet when her daughter was about a month old. By then her daughter's digestive system had calmed down and she could tolerate a wider variety of tastes and compounds in her mom's breast milk.

If cooking isn't your thing, or if a new family needs more meals than friends can provide, you can call on a gourmet meals delivery service. "Food is the most powerful drug we can take," says personal chef, Susan Sears Smith, "And new moms need fresh foods in beautiful abundance."

The menus and particulars of the services vary, but each chef is dedicated to providing wholesome ingredients cooked with skillful care. So move beyond pizza, fast food, and frozen dinners. "The connection between food and health and healing is very important," says Smith. "I like to delight the taste buds and take care of the body."

Setting up a food tree

Use this as a template to create a food tree:

Name

Phone

Email

Availability

Possible meals

Postpartum foods for nursing mothers

Avoid:

- Gas-producing foods such as cabbage, onions, tomatoes, broccoli, fried, and sugary foods
- Beans unless they are part of your regular diet
- Shark, swordfish, king mackerel, and tilefish, may be contaminated with mercury
- Spicy foods (some babies tolerate spicy foods better than others)
- Alcohol
- Caffeinated beverages

Add:

- Lots and lots of water!
- Avoid constipation by including fruits, vegetables, and whole grains in your diet
- Prunes and bran can help if you have a tendency toward constipation
- Iron-rich foods such as red meats, dried beans and peas, or enriched cereals to avoid anemia
- Calcium-rich foods such as milk, yogurt, cheese, cottage cheese, and dark green leafy vegetables.

In the oven: cake designs

There's a particular cake design that's been seen at many Blessingways in my hometown. Lovingly shaped into a round woman giving birth, it evokes laughter and the unusual dilemma of figuring out which part to eat. Some women like to save certain parts for the mother's husband or partner to eat.

When Karen Robinson brought the cake to a friend's Blessingway, it sparked a discussion about how cannibals believe that when they eat an enemy, they are absorbing some of the strength or courage. "We somehow translated that into us taking a part of the mother with us to hold and protect and nurture within ourselves until it was time for the baby to be born, " she explained.

Karen used icing to make glasses and brown hair, personalizing the cake even more. Don't forget to take pictures of the cake!

Whether you decide to order a traditional cake from your favorite bakery or make a one-of-a-kind treat, eating cake together is a ritual shared by many cultures (though most don't make Chocolate Decadence). Special foods serve the ritual purpose of uniting the celebrants in the common act of eating, with all its rich, symbolic associations. It nurtures not only our bellies, but also our spirits. In many cultures, both ancient and modern, rites-of-passage are centered around a shared meal. Cake or other sweets is usually the most important part of the meal (or the only food). Rich foods are meant to be shared—they offer an intimate way to make a connection. In many cultures sweets are not eaten daily but reserved for special occasions—so make your cake unique!

Everyone Makes a Wish

I first did this at a children's birthday party with cupcakes but it works well for any time you're blowing out candles on a cake.

Give each person her or his own candle and together everyone can make their own wish for the honoree and then blow out the candles all together!

Foods can also be a vehicle for communicating information about one culture to another. Food can be a bridge between two people coming from different cultures or for a family adopting a child from another culture or country.

- Muslims celebrate the end of the Ramadan fast (commemorating when the Koran was sent down as a guidance to the people) with a feast. The most important part of the meal is dessert.
- Jewish families begin the New Year (Rosh Hashanah) with a sweet treat. Honey is used liberally, not only in desserts like honey cake, but even to start off their holiday meal by dipping apple wedges in honey.

- Italians were preparing and consuming sweet foods even before the first professional bakers appeared in Rome in the second century BC.

Shapes

If you're looking for a particular shape such as an animal, look through cake-making books for templates. You can also buy heart-or star-shaped cake pans.

To make the birthing women cake:

1. Mix a double batch of you favorite recipe or use two boxes of cake mix.
2. Divide batter into two eight inch round cakes, one cupcake pan, and two loaf pans (at least four-by-nine inches). Make the batter levels the same height in each cake pan.
3. Cool cakes before cutting
4. Cover a large (twenty-four-by-eighteen inches) piece of card-board or lightweight wood with foil.
5. Put one round cake in the center of the board.
6. Use cupcake for baby's head, emerging from mom.
7. Cut down second round cake to make mom's head.
8. Cut the other two cakes into arms and legs.
9. Use a thin layer of frosting to cover the cake, especially the areas where you've cut (this is to prevent crumbs from getting all over mom).
10. Frost generously.
11. Apply face and hair (include pubic and/or underarm hair) details for mom and baby using either a pastry bag or store-bought icing tubes.
12. Spread flowers around the cake.
13. Don't forget to take a picture!

Grace/Blessing

Before you cut the cake or serve the meal, take a moment to say grace or offer a blessing. If you belong to a certain religion, draw from that faith. If you prefer a non-denominational approach, you could do several things:

1. Sing Happy Birthday
2. Hold hands and ask for a moment of silence
3. Offer a blessing such as the one my children taught me:
   Blessings on the sun
   Blessings on the earth
   Blessing on the meal
   Blessings on those we love near and far
   Blessings on our friends and family
   And blessings on (name of the mom)

Mind

Using our minds is what most of us do when we are preparing to become mothers. We read, talk, and think about what our baby is doing as she or he is growing. We read about birth and breastfeeding. We talk to our mothers, friends, and many strangers. Here are a few ideas to keep your mind from spinning too tight or too wildly. By focusing your mind into creating beauty in a poem or blessings, or harnessing it to delve deeply into your visions and dreams of birth and beyond, you can bring this element into balance with your body and soul.

RECORD KEEPING

Journals

Baby books are helpful for recording the milestones of your baby's first year or two. Baby books record the facts but not the feelings. I think that's why so many of us let them collect dust after the first few months. Writing "June twenty-second, weaned from nursing" is not at all the same as, "When he woke at two thirty in the morning and wanted to nurse, I said no. He cried for about fifteen minutes. Then he got out of bed, walked into the kitchen in the dark house and screamed at the refrigerator for his juice. I put water in a tippy cup and handed it to my outraged son, we went back to bed and finally fell asleep."

Writing the stories of your pregnancy, birth, and parenting experiences gives you a much more complete record for yourself and to share with your child. Children love to hear the story of their birth. Writing it down soon after the fact helps you remember all the details. And details are what make a story strong.

New writers often worry that if their ideas aren't bestseller quality, than why write them at all. Do you not take photographs of your child even though you're not a professional? Focus on the little things, the amazement of the first kick you feel, the texture of your newborn's skin, the look on your child's face the first day of kindergarten. Small moments contain big feelings.

You may find that writing about your children triggers memories of your own childhood. Write those stories too. You can learn a lot about the feelings and emotions you have as a parent by looking at how you were raised.

In my writing class for pregnant women, I am constantly amazed at the diversity of stories that all started with the same topic. Although we share many commonalities as parents, each person's experience is uniquely his or her own. Writing reminds us of that.

To get started, buy a special notebook. Hardcover blank books are ideal. Spiral bound ones give you more flexibility in where you write as well as the freedom to include photos or other memorabilia.

To get the creative juices flowing, start with some of these ideas.

1. Write about how you felt when you found out you were pregnant.
2. Tell how you told your husband/partner you were pregnant.
3. Describe the changes your body is going through.

Definitely write the story of your child's birth. Try to get both parents to write their version. You will be amazed how differently two people can see a shared experience.

Once you're a parent, write about some regular event in your child's life such as meals or diaper changes. Try writing it from your child's perspective. Write about your child's favorite toy or food or activity. Write about your family history, religion, and traditions. Tell the story of your child's first birthday. How did you feel? What did you do?

One writing rule does apply, "Show, don't tell." There's a big difference between, "Emily loves music." and " When I came home last night, Emily and her dad played me a duet on the guitar and the harmonica. Two-year-old Emily sang the words, "Oh mama honey, I love you."

Writing the stories now will give you and your family a cherished gift for years to come. Write about your personal experiences as a parent. Then, when your grown child asks if you remember what they were like as a baby, you'll be able to say, "Yes, I do."

Photography

One of the most beautiful things in the world is a pregnant woman. Her body blossoming with the miracle of life, she carries a mystery in her belly. Like a fertility goddess, the archetype of the female, she represents the future of our species.

Hormones and other physiological changes make her skin glow and her hair shine. She becomes round and full.

In our culture, we cover our pregnant women in pink prints and cute overalls. It is rare we ever actually see a pregnant woman's body. Media images of pregnancy and birth have the women in hospital gowns, draped with surgical sheets. But there are many women who give birth naked, uncomfortable from the heat of labor—their self-consciousness gone.

Actress Demi Moore created a stir a decade ago when she posed naked and pregnant for a magazine cover. It was probably the first time in our society most people had seen a pregnant body.

Many couples take pictures of the woman's changing body. Profiles taken monthly document the growing baby. And in the course of nine months, most people take regular snapshots.

Birth is another time we shy away from the camera, and from really looking at a birthing body. I have only a few shots from my first delivery. My second, a home-birth, is well documented. I wanted the photos even if no one else saw them. But I found, when I did show them, the reaction was very positive. My mother-in-law, skeptical of the homebirth was amazed. "I didn't realize how natural giving birth is," she told me. The pictures, along with my story, changed her perspective.

I look back on my first two pregnancies and wish I had taken more pictures of my belly. Posing with my husband on a hiking trail is nice but it doesn't quite capture the goddess within me. I have a few more photos from my second pregnancy but I am always clothed.

With my third and final pregnancy, I made it a priority to be photographed. I realized how powerful an image a pregnant woman is, and I wanted this special time in my life to be recorded in all its glory. I wanted the photos to celebrate and honor my pregnancy with all its stretch marks and sags. I called professional photographer Holly McNutt, who specializes in pregnancy portraits.

"I was intrigued by the pregnant body as a photographer even though I had never seen one before," said McNutt. "The first woman I photographed was a model I hired. I was nervous around her and didn't know what she could do or not do in the natural settings I usually photographed in."

McNutt takes black and white pictures outside in private outdoor settings. It is a perfect blend; demonstrating without words the inherent grace and beauty of a pregnant woman. She does studio portraits as well but I like the use of rocks, trees, and sun providing the backdrop.

The session itself was fun too. I enjoyed the opportunity to feel the wind and sun and even a few drops of rain on my big belly. I felt united with all the women all over the world who give birth naturally, connected to the earth. Sitting on a rock draped only by the sun, I was a creature of the earth and I loved it.

Like looking back on wedding photos, these pictures will remind me of the unique time of my pregnancies. And this third child, so often left out, will be the one I am caressing in the sun on a rock.

BLESSINGS

> *A blessing is not something that one person gives another. A blessing is a moment of meeting, a certain kind of relationship in which both people involved remember and acknowledge their true nature and worth, and strengthen what is whole in one other.*
>
> —Rachel Naomi Remen from *My Grandfather's Blessings: Stories of Strength, Refuge, and Belonging*

Blessings are usually offered at the beginning or end of things. We offer a blessing at meals, weddings, and funerals. But blessings can be offered anytime. They are a sacred pause in our busy lives, no matter who or what you offer your blessing to.

In his book, *Blessing: The Art and the Practice*, author David Spangler suggests, "A blessing can be anytime we wish to make a deeper connection with the life (and lives) around us. As much as it is an invocation, it's also an act of discovering the part of us that moves in harmony on the dance floor of creation. In fact, the art of blessing is not only about the act of blessing but about an attitude towards the world, a way of seeing things that goes beyond our ordinary perceptions."

Historically blessings are part of religion—a holy act if you will. They imply a "belief in things seen and unseen." That implies that a blessing can impact in some way the unseen world. It makes offering a blessing a symbol of our spirituality.

If we take this divine concept to our daily lives, we can see that to bless a person, thing, or event, in essence means to recognize its value and connection to us. When we take the pause and honor that, we bring a positive and powerful reminder of all we are blessed with.

A Mother Blessing may be the first time that you have received a personal blessing. It may be difficult to receive it, but if you can really let it in, it will make a difference in how you parent. It will help you learn to let others in to help you, to support you and to cherish you.

What to say

Family welcome

We welcome our family and friends and say thank you for being here today to celebrate the birth of the newest (family name). We thank this baby for bringing us together in joy. We ask each of you to bless our family, keep us strong, and help us protect, guide, and love this baby throughout his or her life.
Today, we open our hearts to this baby and give her or him a true home. Let us love each other boundlessly and build a strong foundation for our family within these protective walls.

Opening blessing

Blessed Mother, Father, God, Great Spirit
(whatever name you are comfortable using)
Bless this circle of friends and family as we come together to honor (name of honoree).
Bless our hands and hearts as we work together to create beautiful symbols of our love for (name) and her baby.
Bless all the women who have come before us into this tribe of mothers.
We are grateful to be here and thankful for all we have, share, and dream.
Blessed be.

Closing Blessing

The time for leaving draws near. We hold hands and remember the gifts of today—a new life, a new family, and new circle of friends. We give thanks for these gifts and we cherish the times to come when we are together again.

GRATITUDE PRACTICE

It is important not only to be grateful to others but also to be grateful for others. We need to cultivate a gratitude for others' giftedness in the same way that we appreciate a beautiful sunset or a smile from a loved one. Others always seem to have been given gifts in life that we desire, and so it's easy to be envious. Riding sidesaddle with envy is a dangerous practice: I would be happy if I had what he or she possesses. By contrast, giving thanks constantly and in all circumstances liberates us from envy.

—Edward Hays in *The Great Escape Manual*

It's easy to get caught up in the to-do list of your life, especially if you have had a career before you had kids. You're used to managing, scheduling, predicting, and planning your day and your life. But with pregnancy and a new baby, all that will change.

One small thing you can do is to stop and give thanks for both the big and small things in your life—your healthy baby and the fact you brushed your teeth that day, your loving partner, and the smell of your baby's head.

Here are some ways to cultivate gratitude:

1. **Gratitude Journal**. Get a spiral bound journal with blank pages. Make an appointment with yourself every day (right before bed or first thing in the morning work the best) to take a couple of minutes to write three things you are grateful for that day.

   Option: Write down three things that went really well that day. Ask yourself why those good things happened to you? Notice if it was because of something you or someone in your life did. Pay attention to your own role in your happiness.

2. **Gratitude Letter**. Martin E.P. Seligman is one of the founders of Positive Psychology. As part of his work in studying what

makes people feel happy and satisfied, Seligman has found that gratitude is a key component. He encourages his clients to write a letter to someone in their life they have never properly thanked. After writing a detailed letter, he asks them to read it to the recipient, a very intimate and moving experience. He says that when you cultivate a past with positive memories for which you are grateful, that carries over into the present, making you happier. Start by writing a letter to your partner or your parents. You can also write one to your child.

3. **Gratitude Practice**. People from all different religious backgrounds include a spiritual practice of gratitude. For some it's a way of life. Another way to look at it is as a part of the foundation of your family life. Being thankful helps us keep our priorities straight, which helps us make sense out of our lives. To set gratitude in your foundation, practice saying "thank you" for all that you have in your life—the joys and the challenges. Practice gratitude for your home, pets, things, memories, dreams, people, experiences, environment, and your growing family. Literally count your blessings!

LETTER TO YOUR CHILD

One way to align your goals, values, and visions of family life with those of your partner is to write a letter to your baby. Though you may prefer to each write your own, you will deepen your relationship if you do it together.

Try not to over-write your letter. If you write what comes to your mind first, you will capture the qualities most important to you. Mull over your ideas before you write, but then allow the words to flow, without much editing if you can. It doesn't matter if you have run-on sentences or fragments—it is a love letter and the best ones come out of your heart and through your hands without getting caught up in the maze of your mind.

Tell your child why you want him or her. Tell your child what family means to you and how you see your family. Talk about the values you care most about and how you see yourself parenting. Tell your child what your dreams are for them. This does not mean telling him what they should do with his life, but what qualities you hope to impart, such as kindness, generosity, adaptability, respect for nature, or strong body awareness. Write down how you see yourself caring for your child—will you respond quickly to her cries? Will you promise to protect without smothering? Will you share your spirituality on a daily basis?

Baby Pictures

One way to learn more about your values and beliefs about parenting is to delve a bit into your own childhood. Dig out pictures of yourself as a baby. Find the earliest pictures you can. Go through your baby book if your parents made one for you. Look at your picture and think about how your parents felt about you. Were they excited to have you? Were you the first, second, third, or ninth child? What do your pictures tell you? Notice what you are wearing and whether you are being held or in a crib. What do your parents remember about you when you were a baby? Did you cry much? Smile early? Think about how you feel about your childhood and how that affects your decision to become a parent.

Your Birth Story

My mother birthed me alone. She was in a women's hospital in Hawaii not long after it became a state, and birth practices for white women were very doctor-focused, not women-centered. The nurse told her to be a good girl and be quiet, so she tried hard to suppress her cries of pain and fear.

When it was my turn to think about what I wanted at birth and how I wanted to welcome my son, I knew that I did not want to be alone. I hired a birth doula and, unlike my own father, who was sent off to the waiting room, my husband let me squeeze his hand throughout my contractions.

It's hard to say if the reason I wanted my birth to be supported by other women was because of my own entrance to the world and the fear and abandonment my mother felt as she pushed me out of her body. It doesn't really matter if it's provable, if it helps me to make choices for myself. My choices were not reactions to my outrage at how the hospital handled birthing women, but rather informed choices that I knew were in alignment with who I was and what was best for me. I went even further in my second birth when I asked my home-birth midwives not to tell me to push like the nurses in the hospital did, but to allow me to find my own way.

If it's possible, ask your mother about your birth. Were you planned? How did your birth go? Was your mother excited, scared, or prepared?

If your mother is not available to ask, think back on stories about when you were born. Did your grandmother make you a quilt? Did friends send gifts? Were you breastfed? Held a lot? Celebrated and loved?

When you consider your own birth story and how your parents welcomed you, you have more information for deciding what you want, what your values are, and how you feel about your baby.

Here is a template to begin your love letter to your child:

Date______
To: Our baby
From: Your Mom and Dad

Dear Child,

As you near the day when we will be able to hold you in our loving arms, we want to state our commitment to you as your parents. We want to tell you about our dreams for you . . .

DREAM CHILD

As my due date drew near, I started dreaming that I was a sea otter giving birth in a bed of kelp, gently rocked by the sea. My baby slipped out of me like an animal.

My daughter's birth lasted less than an hour and I stood while she emerged from me, wet and slippery from her own private ocean. It felt just like the dream.

Patricia Garfield, dream expert and author of *Creative Dreaming*, says women dream about water throughout their pregnancies." We begin our lives as water creatures, suspended in a sea of liquid within our mother's womb. A pregnant woman is drinking fluids for two, herself and her baby. Small wonder that her dreams overflow with images of water, " she writes.

One midwife reports that at least one-quarter of her pregnant clients report having dreamed about giving birth to an animal or non-human creature.

Pregnant women dream more and have more vivid dreams. They also remember more of them. Dreams can give us information about our fears or anxieties, they can reassure us we are doing fine, they can prepare us for birth and motherhood. Dreams are another way of learning more about ourselves, and they can offer a rich tapestry of images to play with in other art projects.

Names

Sarah woke up in the middle of the night and knew her baby's name. She knew the feeling, it had happened before. When she was six months pregnant with her first child, she dreamed her baby was a boy and that his name was Andrew. Her son, who went by nicknames in his childhood, goes by his dream name now, as he becomes a young man.

Garfield writes, "Pregnant women spend many waking hours contemplating possible names for their babies. Harmonious fits to a last name are weighed as carefully as a child's future education. Family names and fashionable ones are tried on for sound. Meanwhile, in sleep, dreams suggest—and sometimes demand—other choices. In olden times American Indians regarded names given in a dream as having power. Today's parents, too, often find that names arising in a dream hold special resonance for them."

Do the name game described on page 143 as a way of exploring the name your dreams have given you.

Tools for Birth

Dreams and dream-states offer more than interesting conversation. They can also be tools for understanding images and beliefs that work for us. Karin Hoskin, a midwife apprentice, used her client's dream to help her cope with labor: "She had dreams during pregnancy about the baby sliding down a slide into her arms." They used the image as visualization during labor/birth.

Robyn Rathweg's first labor was scary and difficult. Though she wanted a home-birth, she ended up in the hospital. She figured she would have another hospital birth with her second child. She used a dream-like state to connect with her baby. "In a guided visualizing, " she said, "I realized that this child would be OK with a home-birth. I changed my plans and started working with a midwife. This time, the guided meditation revealed to me that the child in my womb was a boy. He was happy, a joker, and a rich forest green color permeated everything. Because of the vivid picture of him, we gave him the middle name of Forest. His birth was extraordinary."

How to keep a dream journal:

1. Keep a spiral notepad, pen and small flashlight right by your bed.
2. Write the date you start on a blank page and leave the book open.
3. Tell yourself that you are going to remember your dreams as you allow yourself to relax into your bed.
4. If you awaken during the night with a dream memory (which pregnant women do a lot), you can use the flashlight to write by so you don't become completely awake. Even writing a couple key words can help jog your memory in the morning.
5. When you wake up, don't move for a moment, and notice if you have any images in your head. You may only get a fleeting image. Write it down.
6. You can also use a small cassette recorder, kept at the bedside, to record your dreams.
7. In the morning, read over what you have written and ask yourself, "Why did I dream this?" Often you will quickly recognize an association with something you have heard, read about, or experienced. Look at your emotional response rather than the actual images.
8. If you were upset or frightened by something in your dream that wouldn't frighten you in waking life, ask yourself why this frightened you in your dream.
9. If you have a recurring dream that upsets you (such as bleeding to death after delivery) talk to your midwife or doctor.

Soul

What true spiritual leaders are asking us in the concepts of acceptance and surrender is one thing only: to accept our unity with all life, and surrender our fantasy of separation.

-Christina Baldwin

I thought I knew what surrendering to motherhood was the first time I gave birth. As the yellow leaves of fall matted my deck in the afternoon rain, I sat on the couch and repeated the word, "surrender." Birth was very near—the birth of my son and of me as a mother. When I went into labor after breakfast a few days later, I said it again, "surrender." When I held him in my arms, I was lost forever to the journey of motherhood.

When I was sixteen, I went backpacking in Yellowstone National Park with a girl friend—we got lost for three days. At the top of a barren mountain, we could see salvation as a ribbon of asphalt glimmering with cars in the maze of forest we had struggled through. We sat for a long time up there, eating the last of the peanut butter and crackers we had. It was the first time I felt a presence greater than myself. To experience it, I had to surrender. It was a relief to let go.

Decades later, my husband and I were in Borneo, waiting for an Iban man to take us in his wooden canoe up river to a longhouse. As the sun got higher, we got scared. "What are we doing—we don't know this man, no one knows where we are—anything could happen," we whispered to each other. When the man, who spoke no English, finally arrived, we bravely got in the boat and he took us to an extraordinary festival. We were the only foreigners there. We had surrendered. I found that place inside of me again.

Kyle was born a year after we bought our first house and began a new life in a different town. Jasper came two years later on the first day of winter. Sabrina was born at home on a hot July evening. Kyle, almost four at the time, gave me sips of water between each contraction. Jasper, eighteen months old, wrapped his father's strong arms around him and just watched. Sabrina was the daughter we all wanted.

I felt like I was back on that mountaintop when I held her. I could almost see that ribbon of hope and knew everything was just as it should be. I was complete. I would not be pregnant again. I had a few minutes of holding her and then the boys climbed on the bed with me. Jasper wanted me to hold him. Kyle wanted me to see the scissors he was going to cut the cord with. They bounced on the bed, ketchup in their hair. Jasper needed his diaper changed. I wanted to just hold my new baby—soak up her smells and skin. I wanted to talk about the birth, get something to eat, take a shower.

I held my daughter as she took her first breaths, my boys leaning on me. I realized that this was the moment of true surrender. I had to surrender to motherhood. It meant not getting to eat for a while, not getting hours to just hold my baby. It meant I couldn't be with my children while I was thinking about the article I needed to write. It would mean that on some days, I might get the groceries home at noon, and not have them put away until five. It would mean I would wish for the patience of a saint and settle for the patience of a dog. My only travels would be to the store and the doctor and maybe the zoo on a really good day.

Surrendering to motherhood would mean that I was finally living in that state where something much bigger than me was happening. I would forever be hopelessly lost and wonderfully saved.

When we make art we surrender to the beauty and truth within us. When we linger in the driveway watching the evening clouds glow pink and stop to breathe it into our hearts, we are surrendering for just a moment. It is not a collapse, not a giving up, but rather a trust in the process.

These activities can all be done at a Blessingway, but I offer them here as a place to play alone or with your beloved. Making art as a group, making a symbol of a collective wish, is one of the most powerful ways we can honor one another as we witness each other's journeys on the path of parenthood. Sometimes, the most transformative art is the art we do alone, safe within our own rooms, secure enough to lay out our soul in a cascade of colors, shapes, and textures.

MOTHER POEMS

I have a secret. Every night there is a poem waiting for me. It's a new one each night, sometimes even two or three. Not all of them are good, but they are all good for me. These poems, the Mother Haikus I write, remind me every night that I am a mother, a writer, and a woman.

My nightly poems are a writing practice, as Natalie Goldberg would say. It is a date I keep with myself, not every night but most of them. As any parent can attest to, time for poetry or stories or even showers is squeezed out from between the dishes and the homework and other jobs. It is one of the shadows of parenthood that, to take for ourselves, we feel like we are taking from someone else—our children, our partners, our friends. But we must do it, and these three lines each night keep us connected to who we are, underneath our stretch marks and heartburn. Sometimes it is all I write that day.

Piles of fatigue
Sit on my bones like dirty dishes
Sighing, sleep whispers

I discovered Mother Haikus when I was complaining of not having time to write for myself and being resentful of all the time it took to parent. I was pregnant with my second child and already felt overwhelmed

I found that I only got to the paper after the kids were dreaming, the dishes done, and the cats fed. I, too, was ready for sleep, but I gave myself three minutes to remember myself. As I began to write, I remembered the haiku form. I loved it as a child and wrote whole haiku books in second and third grade. My spirit remembered how to do them, or at least a version of haiku. Three lines but not a "true" haiku most would say. I called them Mother Haikus because they held my rhythm, the rhythm of my sleeping children, the rhythm of the afternoon stories and snacks, the rhythm of my blood, once joined to theirs. I wrote about my day. I wrote about what was right in front of me. My haikus took me into my breath and breathed through me onto the page. I kept them all in a notebook, spiral bound and lined.

He eats snow like it's God's frosting
In a silver bowl on the kitchen table
The yellow parakeet chirps

Mother Haikus reflect my life. Three lines instead of three journal pages. I can't find time for long journal entries, but I love that poems wait for me every night. As a practice, it teaches me to write from the moment, providing description in only a few words. I could wish for hours in a room of my own to write beautiful prose and poetry, but it will stay a wish for a few more years. For now, I write every day, maybe only three lines, but those words capture my spirit, giving voice to something bigger than myself but something that is also me.

First son starts first grade
With a teacher who likes him
Tonight I can sleep

The classic haiku structure is three unrhymed lines of five, seven, and five syllables. Traditionally, Japanese haiku have a pair of contrasting images, one suggesting presence in time and place and the other a more emotional observation. The masters, such as Basho, often make their setting something in the natural world so it's concrete, not abstract. My poems are full of hot summer nights, prowling cats, and midnight clocks. The third line can be a surprise, adding new energy. But of course, when writing night poems, there are no rules.

Develop a new mothering practice, find the poems in your parenting life and give them a voice on the page. Buy a special notebook just for poetry, and see your life in a new way.

Using Mother Poems at a Blessingway:

Since writing, like drawing, can evoke a feeling of panic instead of excitement in many people, it's best to give your guests a place to start. Poems with a structure like the seventeen syllables of Haiku or the question format of a heart poem, make them great choices for a Blessingway.

Invite everyone to get comfortable so they can write. Offer colored markers and crayons to make the writing itself more beautiful. One person reads the list, giving a few moments for everyone to write his or her answer. Do not talk to one another, it will diffuse the experience. Don't wait for every person to finish every answer—it will disrupt the flow. Write what first comes to mind—allow the soul to speak and ask the internal editor to wait her turn.

Here are some specific ways to start:

1. Mother Haikus
   - Write about one quality you think the mom has or you wish for her.
   - Include mom's name.

Nancy waits for him
Her whole life is blossoming
Dream child emerging

2. Group Poem
    - Brainstorm as a group a list of adjectives that describe the mom-to-be to get your ideas flowing.
    - Each person writes one line. Read it by taking turns in the circle.
    - Write the whole poem out in the mother book.
3. Write a short poem (3-7 lines long) and offer the first line:
    - My heart soars...
    - My friend (name)
    - I offer you...
4. Heart poems
    - Have one person read these questions out loud while everyone writes their answers. Write the first thing that comes to mind. Don't wait for everyone to finish before asking the next question. Then give about ten minutes for everyone to turn his or her list into a poem.
    1. Write the title of your current trimester (or how you see your pregnant friend in this trimester)?
    2. What kind of animal are you right now?
    3. What can you offer yourself or your pregnant/adopting friend?
    4. What kind of weather do you like?
    5. What kind of food are you right now?
    6. Others see you as ________?
    7. You see yourself as ________?
    8. What is your favorite thing to do right now?
    9. What are you worried about for yourself or friend?
    10. What kind of natural environment are you right now?
    11. What do you need right now?

FAMILY MANDALA

A family mandala is a visual commitment to your family. It is a promise to uphold your values, to state your desires, and to create a vision for your future. A family mandala can be a family altar but the nature of an altar is as a focal point for your wishes. It is also changeable due to its non-permanent nature. A mandala is a definite statement about who you are and what you want at the time you create it. It's the big picture of your family. It represents the top priorities you hold for your family.

Creating a family mandala may take some time. Because you choose the top three or four attributes or qualities you want for your family, you have to really think about it, and you have to work with your partner to agree. Each of you (and older kids can join you) can take time to think about and write down the qualities you want your family to cherish and live by.

Be specific—instead of saying you want to spend time together say you want to have dinner together every night or you want to go for a hike or bike ride once a week. Choose three or four main qualities. Any more than that and it will feel like a to-do list rather than a mandala.

Instructions

1. Cut a circle out of a piece of poster board. You can use a large platter as a pattern.
2. Divide the circle into three or four sections.
3. Illustrate or design each section with symbols or sayings that represent your values. For instance, you could put a whale tail to represent your love of the ocean and water sports. A tree could represent your strong roots and giving arms. Certain flowers could mean your willingness to keep facing the seasons of life.
4. Before you glue whatever you've chosen to the board, lay it out and as a family agree on the elements and the layout.
5. To better preserve it, spray or paint a coat of acrylic fixative. If it's all paper, you may be able to pass it through a laminator. If you do, be very careful that all edges are glued down.
6. Hang it up where you will be reminded of who you are as a family.
7. If you want it to look more like a medicine shield, punch a few holes on the bottom, thread ribbon or leather cords through, and hang beads, feathers, toys, or natural objects.
8. Make a hanger at the top by punching two holes and threading another piece of ribbon through.

Elements

1. Flags that represent the countries your family came from
2. Pictures of foods that are common to your ethnicity
3. Pictures that represent first or last names
4. Drawings that depict favorite family events
5. Photos that show family celebrations
6. Objects from nature or small toys, jewelry, or charms

MONSTERS UNDER THE BED

Several years ago, when my youngest was still a toddler, I worked with a personal coach to help me form my writing life. I enjoyed writing about my goals, my dreams, and my journey of becoming a writer, but I had one big fear holding me back. I thought that if I gave myself to writing, I would no longer be able to be a good mother.

I was a writer before I had kids and I wrote professionally throughout my pregnancies and post-partum years. But the truth was that I was in cruise mode, just doing the same assignments I'd been doing for years. I wasn't going anywhere. Cynthia Morris, my writing coach, had us do an exercise. She asked us to write down our biggest obstacle to becoming the writer we wanted to be. Then she made us get up and go into another room. We had to wad up our fear (either literally or figuratively) and throw it out the window and say it out loud, "I release my fear. I can be a good writer and a good mother," I said as I walked through the doorway, leaving my fear behind.

It worked.

Right after that, I started working on my books and publishing a bigger variety of articles in a larger range of publications. I never felt that my children came second to my career. They always come first.

As a pregnant woman, you probably have a fear monster or two lurking under your bed. The thought of birth usually brings up fears such as," I won't be able to handle the pain" or "What if something goes wrong?" Father's biggest fears are about his partner's safety and health. He wonders,"What if something happens to my wife/partner?"

Monsters that aren't tamed can and will impact your birth and mothering. If you don't feel safe while in labor, or have too many traumatic or painful images and fears arise, your muscles will contract, your heart will race, and your body will be coursing with adrenaline. Your body cannot tell the difference between fears that are real and fears that are imagined. That 's why it's so important to work through them before you go into labor.

Release your fears by:

- *Writing them down and burning them*
- *Burying them in the ground (or a pot of dirt)*
- *Putting them in a worry jar with a tight-fitting lid*
- *Assigning your fears to a worry doll, rock, figurine, or action figure*
- *Saying them out loud*

The first thing you have to do is figure out who your monsters are and where they like to hide. Write down your biggest fears. Think about what you hope won't happen. It could be getting a cesarean section or that your baby won't be normal or that you might poop during delivery.

Once you've identified a monster or two, give them a name, then ask yourself what you need to do to make the monster no longer a threat.

Mercer Mayer wrote a delightful children's book called *There's a Nightmare in My Closet.* A little boy is scared of the monster in his closet and he shoots him with a cork gun. The monster cries and is scared of the boy, and by the end they are snuggled in bed together.

Here are some specific ways to make friends with your monsters:

1. **Worry dolls**: You can buy or make little Guatemalan worry dolls. After you name your fear, assign it to a doll. Let the dolls hold the fears and anxieties. By doing so, you can feel safe knowing they are contained, known, accepted. They don't have to be destroyed.

2. **Awaken the Warrior**: You can decrease your anxiety by awakening the powerful parts of yourself. What passion have you left behind? Perhaps it's learning to paint or play piano or learn to ride a horse. Pick one that is doable (sky-diving is not recommend at this time!) and plan one small step you can take toward realizing your dream. It could be getting a book about it at the library, browsing through a community center catalog, joining an on-line chat room, calling some teachers. Awakening the doer within you will help you feel that you can accomplish things, and that you have courage to do what's in your heart.

3. **Gift of Time**: If you are getting depressed about your ability to birth or mother, try offering yourself to someone else. (If your depression is serious–lasts more than a few days, impairs your ability to function, or you have extreme thoughts about death or injury—see your doctor or midwife). Think first about what you have to offer, what your unique gifts are. Perhaps you are a wonderful baker, or love to walk dogs, or enjoy doing errands. Then think about the people in your life and all they do for you and/or others. Then go do or give your gift. Please don't lessen the gifting by talking about how much time and energy it took to do it.

Picture This

Art therapists all over the world use art as a way to both express and explore the inner life. "Art therapy is a non-verbal way to connect with our bodies and souls," said Nora Swan-Foster, a Certified Art Therapist. "I don't analyze the art itself, rather we talk about what you put out there."

Swan-Foster specializes in working with pregnant women. "I choose art materials to match the therapy," she explained. "Different materials elicit different feelings." She offers a variety of materials including paper and paint. Crayons can encourage a childlike approach and bring back memories. Pencils tend to be a tight tool that clients often find narrow and fearful. If a client needs to feel abundance, Swan-Foster pulls out lots of materials. Tearing paper is a metaphor for expressing feelings of loss and anger.

Swan-Foster's clients are mostly women in their childbearing year. She works with them through their pregnancies into their post-partum period. "I believe in early intervention," she said. "By working with their fears and beliefs during pregnancy, their journey into motherhood gets off to a good start."

Making art in a safe setting provides women with a way to connect to their bodies and own inner wisdom. Swan-Foster finds this especially helpful for women who've experienced a pregnancy loss or miscarriage. "It gives them a place to express all their feelings," she said. "Sometimes a woman has paradoxical feelings of both happiness and sadness about a loss. Society might label her crazy. But here, those feelings are acknowledged."

The process of making art takes feelings like anger, sadness, or guilt out of the body and puts them down on paper. It is a way of documenting experiences and feelings.

WHEN YOUR DREAMS BECOME NIGHTMARES

Drawing is used a lot more often in childbirth classes, including my own. Making a visual picture of our feelings and concerns gives them a form, which we can then affect.

In one of my classes, Delaney, a young women who knew her baby had significant issues and health problems, drew a picture of herself on a delivery table with the hospital staff hovering over her, all of them floating in a black background. She told us what was going on for her—her doctors were telling her lots of horror stories and wanted her to come in for an ultrasound twice a week. It was making her wild with fear. I asked her to go back and add something (or redraw) that was healing. She drew a red heart around her and her baby and the staff was off in a corner. She told me later she talked to the doctors and asked why she had to get checked so often, they agreed to fewer tests. She colored over her fears and found her own resources again.

Delaney's son was born with significant special needs. Though she knew there would be problems, she was still overwhelmed by the reality of having a child with disabilities. Her mother and husband (who had their own grief to go through) stayed close, and they all tried to focus on the positives. Her son was an eager nurser, and the natural bonding of breast-feeding helped tremendously. She reached out to her friends and found other parents of children born with special needs. Delaney, like all us parents who raise a child with a disability, periodically goes through a continuum of emotions that include grief, anger, acceptance, and action.

Her son's first birthday was joyfully celebrated. As they brought him a chocolate cupcake lit with a single candle, they passed out cupcakes and candles to all their guests. They asked them each to make a wish for their son as they blew out the candles together. Everyone wrote his or her wish in a scrapbook Delaney had started when he was born.

When Things Go Wrong

Delaney's story touches on the reality that not every baby or mother lives through pregnancy and birth. Many women have experienced miscarriages. Some babies die late in pregnancy or right after birth. Some babies are born with significant medical issues and spend their first days, weeks, even months in the hospital. When a woman loses a child from any one of these reasons, she loses her dreams, hopes, and role of herself as a mother. Though not a common experience, it is a rite-of-passage in its own right. And even though a woman may lose a child, she is still a mother, and any way her community can support and honor that will help her find her footing again.

One of the most beautiful services I have ever attended was to honor Ben, the three-day old son of a friend. Though the parents knew their son had heart defects and would need surgery, they had high hopes that he would be OK. But Ben wasn't strong enough to face surgery. Ben died in his parents' arms. He was dearly loved.

At the ceremony, Ben's parents shared pictures of their son. They told the friends and family gathered the story of his birth and of his death. They passed around a basket of flower petals and asked everyone to take a handful and to scatter them in some place that they thought Ben might have liked. I scattered my rose and lavender petals in my son's playroom among the trucks, trains, and musical instruments.

Ceremonies for loss and death are usually much quieter, simpler events. When people are grieving, they have little energy for party planning. You can adapt many of the suggestions offered in this book. Here are some more simple things you can do to honor women who have lost babies.

- ❖ **Candles**: Ask friends to bring candles as a symbol of lighting the way for the spirit of the child.
- ❖ **Mother Blessing**: Consider offering a quiet, intimate Mother Blessing for a woman on her due date. If the death is at term, she may not be ready. It could be done a year later—the loss of a child is never forgotten.
- ❖ **Dolls**: When one of my friends lost her 6-month-old unborn child, she wanted to add a face to her altar for her son. I gave

her a small, plain cloth doll which she and her older son decorated with white fabric, sewed on a heart, and laid in a bed of moss and leaves.

❖ **Altars**: Pictures, symbols, drawings, candles, or whatever speaks to you can go on your altar. When I witnessed a funeral for a baby in Indonesia, the grandmother fed the baby some soft rice as she softly sang to the child. I'm not suggesting you do this, but I am suggesting that putting on a bottle, a spoon, or a jar of baby food is a lovely symbol of your nourishment.

Mother Blessing Checklist

Element		Who is doing this?
Day and Time	____________	____________
Location	____________	____________
Guest list	____________	____________
Invitations	____________	____________
Menu	____________	____________
Cake	____________	____________
Project	____________	____________
Supplies	____________	____________
Flowers	____________	____________
Music	____________	____________
Altar	____________	____________

Messenger: Sends invitations, handles RSVPs
Hearth-Tender: Takes care of food and decoration arrangements
Conductor: Leads, models, goes first for Blessingway elements
Cherisher: Leads, supplies, models nurturing aspects (hair, feet, hands)
Scribe: Writes down blessings, meanings and gifts during the ceremony
Singer: Plans music, supplies instruments or words for songs, leads songs, chants, toning with voice
Creatrix: Plans, supplies, prepares, explains, models art project/activity
Postpartum Helper: Organizes food tree, makes announcement for front door

Sample Mother Blessing Programs

Donna's Blessingway

INVITATION

Please join Donna in celebrating her journey to motherhood with a Blessingway. Our intention is to surround Donna and her child with our wishes for a safe and fulfilling birth, as well as our blessings for a joyful life.
Please bring a potluck dish to share, a candle, and your written blessings. Your presence is the only gift Donna wants!
Call Mia if you have any questions at 111-2222
July 15th, 6 to 8 pm at 12 Blooming Lane

PROGRAM

Element	Who is doing this part?

1. **Welcoming** — Tara
   Greet out in front of door—pour rose water on hands

2. **Opening the ceremony** — Sofia
   Stand in circle, hold hands, ring bell, say:
   Divine mother, blessed father, beloved friends and family, those with us now in the flesh and those with us in spirit. We are gathered in this sacred circle to honor our dear friend and daughter, Donna, as she takes a sacred journey into motherhood. We are honored to be standing with you. May each of us stand in integrity, grace, and love as we offer our blessings to Donna. Ah-Ho.

3. **Introductions** — Colleen
   Introduce with the names of self, mother, grandmother, and children.

4. **Nurturing the mother** — Sandy
   Foot washing, hand massage, and hair brushing with rosemary oil. As this is going on, go around again with a short story of how you know the mother-to-be, Donna.

5. **Offering your blessings** Colleen
Say blessing, then light candle from the "mother" candle and place in bowl of sand in the center of the circle. If not written down, scribe writes. Extinguish candles by snuffing (blowing out diffuses the energy) when done with this part so mom can use them during labor as a focal point.

6. **Creating a symbol or talisman** Grace
After each woman's turn to offer blessings and candles, she writes one word symbolizing the quality she is offering on the heart shaped paper in the basket. Then she hangs it on the ribbon made of fake pearls to hang in Donna's bedroom.

7. **Completion** Sofia
Hold hands in circle again in silence for a minute. Then say:
Thank you divine mother, blessed father, friends and family both near and far for joining us to celebrate, honor, and support our friend Donna. We have shared our stories, laughed and cried together. We have filled Donna with our blessings and given her the lights from within our own hearts to light her way. We have strung our hearts together to encircle her with our love and support. We honor you Donna, as we welcome you to motherhood.

8. **Feasting** Jean

Supplies

- Rose water, bowl, and towels
- Altar, throne, and tissue
- Warm water in a bowl, oils or lotion, brush, towels
- Large broad bowls with fine, clean sand, lighter
- Basket with precut hearts, hole punched through, ribbon to hang
- Mother book, pens, markers, glue to glue in cards
- Camera
- Cups, dishes, etc. for eating

II. Annette's Mother Blessing

INVITATION

A Mother Blessing
For
Annette Miller
Saturday, September 7, 2002
4:00 to 6:30 p.m.
12 Blooming Lane
Boulder, Colorado
Please bring a special bead and a small candle that can be safely held
A light supper will be served
RSVP by September 1
Sherry Miller (303) 111-2222

PROGRAM

Element	Who is doing this part?

1. **Welcoming** — Julie & Shelly
   Meet at front door, remove shoes, ask for silence as they enter the living room and take a seat. Light candle.

2. **Opening the ceremony** — Tracy
   In silence, beat drum three times slowly. Then Tracy leads with a deep breath and a long 'ohm' three times. Then say: *Thank you all for your silence present and your powerful voices. This circle is a circle of support for our friend and sister Annette, as she becomes a mother for the second time. We are here to offer Annette our heartfelt blessings and timeless support. She has asked us to help her build a safe container so she can create a strong, healthy home for her growing family. We are here.*

3. **Introductions** — Kim
   Each woman says her name and then "*I am here for you, Annette.*"

4. **Nurturing the mother** — Janine
   Put Annette in center, support with pillows or people, everyone lays on hands while singing a lullaby.

5. **Offering your blessings** Jessie

Jessie starts and then we go around the circle with each woman offering her blessings as she strings her bead. Jessie goes and kneels in front of Annette as she makes her offering. Judy is the scribe.

6. **Creating a symbol or talisman** Jessie

Jessie ties a knot on one end of a smooth red leather cord. Each woman puts a knot between her bead and the next bead. When it's done, each woman holds it in her hands and fills it with her love. Then it's tied around Annette's neck and she has a turn to respond.

7. **Completion** Tracy

The women stand in the circle; Tracy beats the drum three times. She then say's loudly, *We are here for you, Annette,* and the women repeat the phrase as they raise their hands together in a rush of fun energy.

8. **Feasting** Laurel

Supplies

- Lighter, baking soda (for stray flames)
- Drum
- Birth necklace beads and long cord
- Mother Book

III. Sarah's Blessingway for Adoption

INVITATION

You are invited to a Mother Blessing ceremony for Sarah as she prepares to become a mother. Please bring:
A bouquet of flowers
A packet of your favorite flower seeds
A potluck dish (something "springy")
A blessing for Sarah. She will have a book you can write in or glue something in
RSVP to Tammy at 111-2222 by March 11th
March 14th, 6 to 9 pm (or later) at 12 Blooming Lane

PROGRAM

Element	Who is doing this part?

1. **Welcoming** — Sharon

   Meet at door, music playing, and fabric draped across door. Sharon gathers flowers and puts in water. Women greet and talk to each other.

2. **Opening the ceremony** — Tammy

   Tammy asks Sarah to go into her bedroom. The other women first decorate Sarah's chair with fabric, ribbons and few flowers and then create two rows and put their hands together with the woman across from them to make an arch. They sing as Sarah slowly walks through the arch of hands and then sits in the "throne" prepared for her. They all sit in a circle.

3. **Introductions** — Kathy

   Kathy welcomes the women and asks them to introduce themselves by answering the questions: What is your favorite flower and why?

4. **Nurturing the mother** — Sierra

   While they are answering the introduction question, Sierra leads the group in weaving a crown of flowers for Sarah. One woman arranges the extra flowers. They also massage Sarah's hands and feet and brush her hair.

5. **Creating a symbol or talisman** — Darcy

   Eileen and Tammy have set up a painting space in the kitchen. They have acrylic paints and brushes, smocks and paper towels. Eileen asks them to begin painting their pots in silence. They work together for about fifteen minutes painting, then wash up. They also paint the name of their flower seeds and their own name on a Popsicle stick. While the pots are drying, they sit back in the circle and share their seeds with Sarah. She has time to respond.

6. **Offering your blessings** — Eileen

   After they have painted the flower pots, the women share their blessings by sharing the qualities of the seeds and flowers they choose for Sarah. In the center of the circle is a larger pot with soil in it. As they share, they drop a few seeds into the community pot.

7. **Completion** Kathy
Kathy plays a song and they all get up and dance. Kathy leads them gently by encouraging them to feel the spring in their own step, to smell the fresh dirt, to notice what is blooming in their own hearts. When the song has ended, they come together in a circle, breathe together, and end with a *whoppee*!
(After pots have dried, they need to be sprayed with an acrylic coating before planting.)

8. **Feasting** Darcy

SUPPLIES

- Vases, water, scissor to trim stems
- Three two-inch wide, three-foot long strips of cloth (old sheets work well)
- Clay pots, shovels, potting soil
- Painting supplies (pots, paints, brushes, smocks, water, rags, protected area)

Resources

Books

BLESSINGWAYS/RITUALS

Cortlund, Lucke, Miller Watelet, *Mother Rising: The Blessingway Journey into Motherhood*, Seeing Stone Press, 2004

Cotner, June, *Baby Blessings: Inspiring Poems and Prayers for Every Stage of Babyhood*, Harmony Books, 2002

Dunham, Carroll and others, *Mamatoto: A Celebration of Birth*, Penguin, 1993

Gosline, Andrea Alban, *Welcoming Ways: Creating Your Baby's Welcome Ceremony with the Wisdom of World Traditions*, Cedco Publishing Company, 2000

Hopkins, Jill, *Welcoming the Soul of a Child*, Kensington Books, 1999

Jackson, Deborah, *With Child: Wisdom and Traditions for Pregnancy, Birth and Motherhood*, Chronicle Books, 1999

Shinoda Bolen, Jean, *The Millionth Circle: How to Change Ourselves and the World: The Essential Guide to Women's Circles*, Conari Press, 1999

PREGNANCY

Davis, Elizabeth, et al, *Heart & Hands: A Midwife's Guide to Pregnancy & Birth*, Celestial Arts, 2004

England, Pam, CNM, MA and Horowitz, Rob Ph.D., *Birthing From Within: An Extra-Ordinary Guide to Childbirth Preparation*, Partera Press, 1998

Goldberg, Bonnie (editor), *The Spirit of Pregnancy: An Interactive Anthology for Your Journey to Motherhood*, Contemporary Books, 2000

Menelli, Sheri L (editor), *Journey to Motherhood: Inspirational Stories of Natural Birth*, White Heart Publishing, 2004

Louden, Jennifer, *The Pregnant Woman's Comfort Book*, HarperSanFrancisco, 1995

Osnes, Beth, *Twice Alive: A Spiritual Guide to Mothering Through Pregnancy and the Child's First Year*, Woven Word Press, 2005

Steingraber, Sandra, *Having Faith: An Ecologist's Journey to Motherhood*, Berkeley Publishing Group, 2003

Stern, Ellen Sue, *Expecting Change: The Emotional Journey Through Pregnancy*, Poseidon Press, 1986

BIRTH

Kitzinger, Sheila, *Rediscovering Birth*, Pocket Books, 2000

Kitzinger, Sheila, *The Complete Book of Pregnancy and Childbirth*, Alfred Knopf, 2003

Goer, Henci, *The Thinking Woman's Guide to a Better Birth*, Perigee, 1999

Salt, Karen, *A Holistic Guide to Embracing Pregnancy, Childbirth, and Motherhood: Wisdom and Advice from a Doula*, Perseus, 2003

Korte, Diana and Scaer, Roberta, *A Good Birth, A Safe Birth: Choosing and Having the Childbirth Experience Your Want*, The Harvard Common Press, 1992

Simkin, Penny, *The Birth Partner* (second edition), Harvard Common Press, 2001

MOTHERHOOD

Maushart, Susan, *The Mask of Motherhood: How Becoming a Mother Changes Our Lives and Why We Never Talk About It*, Penguin Books, 1999

Krasnow, Iris, *Surrendering to Motherhood: Losing Your Mind, Finding Your Soul*, Hyperion, 1997

Lamott, Anne, *Operating Instructions, Balantine, 1994*

Kline, Christina Baker, editor, *Child of Mine: Writer's Talk About the First Year of Motherhood*, Hyperion, 1997

Stern, Daniel, M.D., and Bruschweiler-Stern, Nadia, M.D., *The Birth of a Mother: How the Motherhood Experience Changes you Forever*, BasicBooks, 1998

Gore, Ariel, *The Hip Mama's Survival Guide*, Hyperion, 1998, *Mother Trip*, Seal Press, 2000, *and Breeder*, Seal Press, 2001

Hanson, Rick, Ph.D., Hanson, Jan, L.Ac, and Pollycove, Ricki, M.D. *Mother Nurture: A Mother's Guide to Health in Body, Mind, and Intimate Relationships*, Penguin Books, 2002

Goode, Caron B., Ed.D., *Nurture Your Child's Gift: Inspired Parenting, Beyond Words*, Beyond Words, 2001

ADOPTION

Siegel, Joan L. & Solonche, Joel, *Peach Girl: Poems for a Chinese Daughter*, Grayson Books, 2002

CREATIVE EXPRESSION

Fox, John, *Finding What You Didn't Lose: Expressing Your Truth and Creativity Through Poem-Making*, Jeremy P. Tarcher, 1995

Linn, Denise, *Altars: Bringing Sacred Shrines Into Your Everyday Life*, Ballantine Wellspring, 1999

Le Van, Marthe, *Making Creative Cloth Dolls*, Lark Books, 2002

Roth, Gabrielle, *Sweat Your Prayers: Movement as Spiritual Practice*, Putnam Books, 1997

Website Resources from Mother Blessings:

MUSIC

BIRTH: Melissa Michaels and Friends
Wild Life Productions

surf@BDanced.com
1-877-B-DANCED
www.bdanced.com

CREATIVITY COACH

Cynthia Morris
303-442-0664
www.originalimpluse.com

BIRTH INTUITIVE

Teresa Robertson, RN, CNM, MSN, Birth Intuitive
303-258-3904
Teresa@BirthIntuitive.com
www.BirthIntuitive.com

HENNA ARTISTS

Jessica McQueen
805-732-9350
www.hennacaravan.com

Luma R. Brieuc
Professional henna-artist
www.lumanessence.com

CREATIVE DREAMING

Patricia Garfield, Ph.D.
Author of Creative Dreaming
Co-founder and President (1998-9), The Association for the Study of Dreams
www.patriciagarfield.com

DOULAS

Karen Robinson, Intern Midwife
303-665-7997
robinsonkl@gmail.com

WATSU:

David Sawyer, MA, LPC
Intergrative Aquatic Therapy
303-440-9725
d.sawyer@comcast.net

PSYCHOTHERAPIST SPECIALIZING IN BIRTH

Nora Swan-Foster, MA, ATR-BC, LPC
Candidate Analyst in Training with IRSJA
303-595-1006
www.Swanfoster.com

OTHER

Becoming Mothers
www.becomingmothers.com

Jenny Hatch
Mother Blogger, www.NaturalFamilyBLOG.com
www.NaturalFamilyCo.com - Healthy Families Make A Healthy World!

About Rita Loyd, the Cover Artist

As a self taught artist, inspiration to paint Spirit Nurturing Art came to me during a long chronic illness. As my life slowly narrowed around me from lack of physical strength and panic attacks, my ego had no other choice than to step aside, and allow the voice of my spirit to emerge and comfort me through my artwork.

In my artwork I am guided to paint images that encourage me to grow as a spiritual being. To find the inspiration to paint such images I go through a process of self examination to explore where I need the most encouragement. I do this with a mind set of non-judgment in order to not fall into a state of self defensiveness which may hinder my ability to be honest with myself.

As I acknowledge where in my life it is not flowing well, I am able to explore the answers and paint from the wisdom I have gathered.

Once I have finished a painting it then becomes a reminder of my truth and a tool for empowering visualization.

I believe it was through sickness that I was allowed to become whole,for it is in the silence and stillness that the Spirit can be heard.

See more ART by Rita Loyd at www.nurturingart.com

Contact Rita Loyd for a free brochure of Nurturing Art Greeting Cards, rita@nurturingart.com or call 256-880-3935